PSYCHIC
HEALING

Other Books by Sylvia Browne

Adventures of a Psychic (with Antoinette May)
Astrology Through a Psychic's Eyes
Blessings from the Other Side (with Lindsay Harrison)
Contacting Your Spirit Guide (book-with-CD)
Conversations with the Other Side
Exploring the Levels of Creation
Father God
If You Could See What I See
Insight (with Lindsay Harrison)
A Journal of Love and Healing (with Nancy Dufresne)
Life on the Other Side (with Lindsay Harrison)
Meditations
Mother God
The Mystical Life of Jesus
The Other Side and Back (with Lindsay Harrison)
Past Lives, Future Healing (with Lindsay Harrison)
Phenomenon
Prayers
Prophecy (with Lindsay Harrison)
Psychic Children (with Lindsay Harrison)
Secrets & Mysteries of the World
Secret Societies . . . and How They Affect Our Lives Today
Spiritual Connections
Sylvia Browne: Accepting the Psychic Torch (anthology)
Sylvia Browne's Book of Angels
Sylvia Browne's Book of Dreams (with Lindsay Harrison)
Sylvia Browne's Lessons for Life
Temples on the Other Side
Visits from the Afterlife (with Lindsay Harrison)

The ***Journey of the Soul*** Series
(available individually or in a boxed set)

God, Creation, and Tools for Life (Book 1)
Soul's Perfection (Book 2)
The Nature of Good and Evil (Book 3)

All of the above are available at your local bookstore,
or may be ordered by visiting:
Hay House USA: **www.hayhouse.com®**
Hay House Australia: **www.hayhouse.com.au**
Hay House UK: **www.hayhouse.co.uk**
Hay House South Africa: **www.hayhouse.co.za**
Hay House India: **www.hayhouse.co.in**

PSYCHIC
HEALING

Using the Tools of a Medium
to Cure Whatever Ails You

Sylvia Browne

HAY HOUSE, INC.
Carlsbad, California • New York City
London • Sydney • Johannesburg
Vancouver • Hong Kong • New Delhi

Published and distributed in the United States by: Hay House, Inc.: www.hayhouse.com • *Published and distributed in Australia by:* Hay House Australia Pty. Ltd.: www.hayhouse.com.au • *Published and distributed in the United Kingdom by:* Hay House UK, Ltd.: www.hayhouse.co.uk • *Published and distributed in the Republic of South Africa by:* Hay House SA (Pty), Ltd.: www.hayhouse.co.za • *Distributed in Canada by:* Raincoast: www.raincoast.com • *Published in India by:* Hay House Publishers India: www.hayhouse.co.in

Editorial supervision: Jill Kramer • *Design:* Jen Kennedy

Library of Congress Cataloging-in-Publication Data

Browne, Sylvia.
  Psychic healing : using the tools of a medium to cure whatever ails you / Sylvia Browne. -- 1st ed.
      p. cm.
  ISBN 978-1-4019-1088-4 (hardcover : alk. paper) 1. Mental healing. I. Title.
  RZ400.B776 2009
  615.8'51--dc22

                        2008027478

Tradepaper ISBN: 978-1-4019-1090-7
Hardcover ISBN: 978-1-4019-1088-4

13 12 11 10   5 4 3 2
1st edition, February 2009
2nd edition, April 2010

Printed in the United States of America

For all my loved ones and clients
who say they pray for me
as they know I pray for them,

and

for Sister Emmanuel, a Carmelite nun
whom I love dearly
and whose prayers I treasure.

Contents

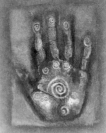

Preface

As long as humankind has existed, so has the practice of healing. Oral and recorded histories tell us that the earliest human beings prayed to their deities to keep them well, and they even made sacrifices in order to ward off the evil that was thought to enter the body and cause illness. From shamans and witch doctors to herbalists and holy people, they practiced their religions, witchcraft, or alchemy—by using amulets, charms, potions, herbs, spells, and invocations—to summon the good that would overcome evil and heal the sick.

Thousands of years ago, it was believed that ailments came about from demons entering the body; in Shakespeare's day, "bad humors" were to blame for poor health. Such notions led to the practice of bloodletting, which was supposed to balance the body's humors or rid it of any bad spirits that may have entered it. It was such a common practice that even George Washington was repeatedly bled by the doctors who were treating his maladies at the end of his life.

Recent history has seen incredible advances in conventional medicine, but holistic therapies have also made their way into our culture. Several of the ingredients in our new drugs come from rare plants in the rain forests that have been used by native healers for centuries. Countless individuals also look for the answer for wellness in crystals, Reiki, the laying on of hands, acupuncture, or herbal and natural remedies. And then there are past-life regressions, which have been so successful in releasing the traumas we carry over in our morphic resonance (which we'll discuss later) that make us phobic and sick in *this* life.

The many healing arts are too numerous to mention, and many of them are, in fact, bogus. People from the United States routinely go to Mexico, Switzerland, and the Philippines for exotic treatments, and the lines to visit Lourdes in France are staggering—all based on the hope of a miraculous cure. Do I believe in miracles? You bet . . . I see them almost every day. But I'm firmly against empty promises and occult gadgetry. I think that we have to approach everything with an open mind, but when you start to deplete your life savings for the pledge of some quack, then you'd better run.

The older I get, the more convinced I become that it's not just genetics or germs alone that cause health problems. Yes, illness may play a part in our chart (that is, the life plan we've chosen to help us learn and advance our soul), but more times than not, it's other people and external situations that are responsible for making us sick. The strain becomes so unbearable that our immune system's natural defenses go down, and then our body becomes an open portal for all manner of ailments and carryovers from this existence or past ones. We can't eliminate stress altogether, nor would we want to, because there are bad kinds *and* good kinds. Good stress results when we notice that our hard work has paid off; bad stress comes when we're on a treadmill of survival, with no light at the end of the proverbial tunnel. If we can't find some comfort or joy in life, we can rest assured that illness will follow.

Why do you suppose some people go into remission from disease and others don't? Sure, it has a lot to do with our wonderful modern medicine, but like one of my doctors told me, "We're only the technicians—you govern your own cure." I wholeheartedly believe this, that the healing process almost always begins with the patient and his or her willpower.

My grandmother took that view a step further, insisting that one's will could overcome anything. That's a little extreme, but for her it seemed to work. For example, she broke her hip when she was 84 years old. The doctor set it, and when she demanded to go home, he reluctantly let her (no one would have tried to face her down when she was angry). The next day I went to see her and found her pushing a chair in front of her, hobbling about. I said, "Grandma, for God's sake—lie down." She replied, "That's just foolishness!"

Even though the doctors said that by leaving the hospital early, blood clots could have killed her, my grandmother went on to live for five more years. She walked a little haltingly, but that was it. I'm not advocating what she did; I'm merely stating what I've witnessed, not only with her, but with countless others as well. So many times I've seen those who have been given a death sentence set their will on a greater purpose and subsequently overcome the illness or disease to survive to a ripe old age.

Now, as I like to say at lectures, "If you're sick, use both established and alternative methods of healing. The field of medicine has some wonderful practitioners, and a few bad ones, too—but that's the case with any profession." So in no way do I mean for you to stop getting your checkups and physicals every year or seeing your physician if you have a problem. Take your green tea, vitamins, and herbs if you want; but to rule out conventional medicine is just plain stupid. You don't treat a problematic gallbladder with grape seed extract and skip seeing your doctor . . . how idiotic is that? Use your common sense and remember that God made doctors to help you.

Just as I say not to negate traditional medicine, don't dismiss alternative treatments either—in other words, you have options, so utilize them all to your best advantage. Holistic medicine includes some great treatments, just as conventional medicine does. Prayer, meditation, hypnosis, acupuncture, nutrition and diet, and herbs and supplements are all holistic treatments that have proven to be quite successful.

I've written this book to assist any of you who can be healed from illness due to cell memory or mental disharmony, which are very similar, for one can trigger the other and vice versa. Cell memory and mental disharmony may be behind most maladies, but negativity causes them to activate. It also helps if you take stock of the people and situations surrounding you and decide what sets off your anxieties.

My intent is to give you ways to heal yourself with the aid of your doctor(s), as well as provide preventive-maintenance advice that will ensure a healthy life. I want to emphasize that you should try to eat well, engage in some exercise, and keep joy and positive thoughts in your mind, as these effects go a long way toward wellness. Keep your will strong; believe in miracles; and most of all, know that God can heal . . . if you're just open to it.

❦ ❦ ❦   ❦ ❦ ❦

Introduction

I have found that almost all illness comes from one of three factors: (1) cell memory, (2) mental disharmony, or (3) as part of our charts. When we're on the Other Side, we determine what we want to learn and experience for God and our own souls. Then before we incarnate, we map out our goals for that particular life, along with any obstacles we'll need to overcome or endure. Since everybody who lives must also die, we chart our death and the circumstances of it as well. Some of us may chart to perish in an accident, others from old age, and still others from warfare or violence; yet many choose to die from illness or disease.

If we've written being sick into our charts to experience it, this doesn't mean that we're unable to be healed, for we might have also written *that* into our charts. There are cases, however, when people write in an illness to experience and learn from—but they also put in that they won't recover. As fatalistic as this may seem, such individuals aren't meant to be cured, nor do they want to be, at least on a soul level.

Always keep in mind that you can't interfere with what others want to learn because they've chosen their own paths. On the positive side, only advanced souls put difficult challenges into their charts, for they can handle them more successfully than others can. You also must realize that even a life of pain and suffering is transient—the Earth plane is just a school where human beings can learn about negativity in all forms and is temporal in nature when compared with eternity.

If you've indeed chosen to contract an illness and die from it, there's not much that any type of healing can do to stop it. However, since you can't know for sure if you *did* write it into your chart, it's best to assume that you didn't—attack any malady with that attitude in mind. If you don't at least try to heal yourself, there's absolutely no chance of being cured. It's like saying that if you don't put food in your mouth, you can't eat.

Science tells us that illness and disease come from "germs" or "viruses" that invade our bodies. While this is true, it doesn't go far enough and take in the "big picture," so to speak. Germs and viruses certainly do contribute to poor health, but the *cause* is much larger in scope. What makes one person more susceptible to being sick than another?

While scientists will say that some individuals have fewer antibodies to fight things off or aren't "immune" to certain afflictions because of their DNA makeup, that doesn't explain why some people have this particular DNA or cell structure while others don't. They may say that it's due to heredity or "good genes," but they're still missing the boat because everyone basically has the same construction components within their bodies. In other words, all human beings have the same capability to battle whatever may compromise our health, but some don't activate that capability as well as others do. Why? It's the result of the combination of not knowing how to do it, not being aware of alternative or preventive treatment methods, and not keeping the mind healthy in its outlook and optimal functions. This may sound confusing, but it really isn't.

You see, most of us don't know how to stimulate our own defenses to prevent illness. Sure, we know little things, such as keeping our environment and body clean (washing our hands to eliminate germs, cleaning our counters, and so forth) or isolating ourselves from those who are infected (wearing masks and rubber gloves, sterilizing, quarantining, and the like), but how do we reach our *inner* defense systems? Science tells us that such systems activate by themselves almost autonomously (such as when white blood cells attack infection), but this isn't always enough, and we often get sick anyway. It's like sending out a squad of ten soldiers to combat an army of thousands. We need a battalion of *hundreds* of thousands to fight for us! We can do this by programming—and deprogramming—our minds and bodies, as we'll see throughout the following pages.

Unfortunately, one of the bureaucratic problems with medicine is that it is a reactionary practice: that is, a person gets sick and the doctor reacts by trying to treat the symptoms. Very little of medicine is devoted to prevention, except in the areas of research or serum development. We're seeing a bit more preventive care in the fields of geriatrics and nutrition, but even here, change comes at an extremely slow pace. And while there's historically been a general disdain in Western medicine for holistic practices, this is thankfully changing for the better.

As for encompassing treatments for cell memory and conflicts of the conscious and subconscious minds, there really aren't any. A few doctors I work with are exploring this in limited usage, and psychiatry does delve into the subconscious mind and its workings to a point, but further therapies need to be developed and used in order to help patients. I find it funny that psychiatry isn't in the foreground of keeping the mind healthy and working optimally, but again, this is a reactionary field. Psychiatrists deal with patients who are exhibiting symptoms that need to be corrected, but they rarely attempt to prevent these symptoms from occurring in the first place. It isn't their fault, just as it isn't the fault of doctors in any reactionary field. This is just the way conventional medicine is set up and how it operates (no pun intended).

There's hardly any work being done in preventive medicine in this arena, except for the numerous self-help volumes out there, which do benefit many. So one of the reasons I've written this book is to present and discuss some additional treatment methods. I want you to thoroughly understand that keeping the mind healthy is a matter of learning how to maintain a positive attitude—and adjusting to life's problems by changing the way you live and think.

❧ ❧ ❧

Not long ago I was talking to my spirit guide Francine about healing, and I was once again shown that if you ask the right questions, you'll get the answers you seek. It's also reassuring to find out that even on the Other Side (also known as heaven, this is our true Home and reality), we never know everything—we're always in a state of euphoric discovery. It makes me nervous when I hear people say that they "know it all," since that's an occult and devastating ego trip.

If you're unfamiliar with Francine, please allow me to introduce her to you. She's been with me since I was born and is my primary spirit guide. (I also have a secondary guide, Raheim, who came to me when I was in my 30s, and I'll talk more about him later on in this book.) While I am clairvoyant, I also happen to be clairaudient, so I actually hear Francine speak. In addition, I'm a trance medium, so she uses my body to communicate from time to time. Francine is what's called "a control," which is a term used to describe the spirit guide of a full trance medium. This term was coined in the heyday of Spiritualism because the spirit guide actually controlled who would come into the medium's body.

Trance mediums give up their bodies to be occupied by entities in spirit form, allowing passed-over loved ones, guides, and others with messages to impart to come into them to communicate. Francine, however, makes sure that only compatible entities enter into my body because she knows that an entity with different energy coming in could take a great toll on me. I've always trusted her in this, and she's never failed to put my health and well-being above everything else.

Here's what my spirit guide recently let me know:

1. The human mind builds and heals, so you can easily address the cause of your maladies and your own healing ability. If you're ill, ask for infused knowledge from your spirit guides and master teachers, but also be aware of what you say to yourself. And find what patterns or influences are physically or mentally causing any disorder or struggle, be they external (coming from society, morals, religion, family, relationships, or jobs) or internal (fears, phobias, compulsions, obsessions, anxieties, or neuroses). Resolve the conflict within, and remember that *where there is harmony, there can be no conflict.* What are your feelings and attitudes about your situation?

2. You are the authority of what you feel and what you've been through. Francine stressed that you need to research what your illness is about—reconstruct, rebuild, normalize, optimize, and maximize the affected portion of your body. Instruct and even command your body to restructure its perfect shape, which your DNA knows. Tell the major functions and organs how they should behave, since they're sentient. If there are foreign or alien materials, they must be removed and excreted without damage to the surrounding healthy tissue.

It's very important to note here that *people must want to be healed!* You cannot interrupt or intercept others' charts if they've elected to learn through illness.

3. Your mind has the power to heal itself, and your body knows how to be well. Each cell in your body knows and remembers the proper way to be healthy.

Neither my spirit guide nor I *ever* advocate that you disobey your doctor's advice! However, do keep in mind that some traditional treatments bring financial gain with them—hospitals make a fortune on chemotherapy, for instance. And while Western medicine considers the placebo a sham, it can be the most powerful tool for healing on this planet, particularly when you realize that millions of people are in spontaneous remission from cancer without taking a single drug.

When it comes to horrible diseases such as cancer, it can really help to get your mind to a quiet place and then go into the pain and say, "I'm in control." For particularly agonizing conditions, such as multiple sclerosis (MS), try visualizing that you've put the ailment into a big red ball, placed that ball in a safe or some other enclosed container, and blown it up! If you have strange illnesses or undiagnosed distresses, ask yourself, "What's going on in my life? What happened prior to my getting sick?"

Things will get better. For example, if the flu is going around, you can stop it quickly by programming away from it. But be sure to speak directly to specific areas in your body rather than being too general. Internal organs are sentient: they have cognition and self-recognition, they have a direct connection to the brain, and they can think and act independently. You'll want to tell any cells that have gone haywire to go back to their flawless form—each body part knows what it should be from conception because of DNA. Of course if there was a defect from birth, it was preplanned and charted for your soul's perfection and learning. But you can address whatever isn't congenital with cell memory . . . every part of your body can talk to you, and you can talk to it.

A Medium's Gifts

Since the title of this book is *Psychic Healing,* I'd like to explain the concept in detail. As I've already touched upon, I plan to deeply explore the notion that we can all heal ourselves with our minds. However, the title is also a play on words because I *am* a psychic. I'll share the tools of my mediumship in these pages, particularly the advice Francine and Raheim have communicated to me, to help you optimize your wellness.

But first let me give you a quick primer on mediumship, for we don't all have the same talents or work the same way. I've been told by various researchers who have tested me that I have more inherent abilities than the average medium. Most psychics have been given one or even two of the following gifts: some can communicate with the dead on the Other Side; some can see the ghosts that still roam on *this* side; some are clairvoyant (they can see future, past, and present events); some are clairaudient (they can hear their guides); some are trance mediums (such as Edgar Cayce, Margaret Leonard, and Arthur Ford); some are physical mediums (they use kinetic energy to move objects or create manifestations or heal); some are healers (such as Padre Pio); and some use various skills such as psychometry (getting vibrations and knowledge from inanimate objects), astral travel, and channeling (getting feelings and impressions from a guide or spirit). All of these abilities are a part of the mystical world; while most legitimate psychics and even laypeople may be able to utilize one or more of them, they often choose not to do so, either out of fear or a lack of commitment or skill.

Psychics do vary in ability and talent . . . and some also vary in their own spirituality, character, honesty, and purpose. For example, I found in my extensive research that Eusapia Palladino was a very famous physical medium who'd proven to countless researchers that she could move objects with her mind. However, I also found out that she was not above cheating when she had to: when caught, she would explain tearfully that sometimes she wasn't able to maneuver items at will, so out of fear of rejection, she'd lend a foot or hand to do so. This is interesting in that it highlights that not all psychics (especially physical mediums) are able to manifest their abilities all the time. In observing other psychics at work, I've found that some are really "on" at times and have innumerable "hits" that indicate paranormal ability, yet on other occasions, these same mediums can be completely wrong. Although parapsychology is a recognized science, psychic ability is not an *exact* science, and I don't know if it ever will be.

Speaking for myself, I've found that there are instances when my gifts seem to manifest better than at others—in other words, I can pick up anything and everything at times with seemingly no effort, while at other times, I have to really work to receive impressions, communication from spirits, or clairvoyant insights. It has nothing to do with how I feel mentally or physically, because I've been sicker than a dog and had my abilities perform fantastically. I'm convinced that I don't get a lot from some people because they're either boring or don't have much going on in their lives. I think that mediums connect with the energy and souls of others, and if there isn't much there, they have to strive harder to find it.

I'm blessed to have more than one psychic gift: I'm clairvoyant, clairaudient, and a trance medium; I can see and communicate with spirits and ghosts; I can get vibrations from objects (psychometry); I can astral travel (although I don't particularly care for it); I can hear and communicate with plants; I can channel; and I can heal. About the only talent that hasn't manifested in me is that of kinetic energy or being a physical medium. I'm told that I'm one of the few trance mediums in the world today, and I believe that's because most psychics don't want to give up their bodies to other entities and choose to channel instead. Yet even though I've been given more gifts than most people, I don't pat myself on the back. God made me this way . . . besides, my ego doesn't work like that. I do believe in my abilities, or else I wouldn't be out there trying to help others, but there are also many other good psychics. (Come to think of it, though, there are many not-so-good ones, too.)

Full trance mediumship is a dying art, as there are few today who have the ability to do it. In the heyday of Spiritualism, there were quite a few of them, along with plenty of con artists who weren't above using trickery and outright fraud to fool grief-stricken people into thinking that they were communicating with passed-over loved ones. One of the great debunkers of all time was, believe it or not, the magician Harry Houdini.

Houdini was convinced that there was an afterlife, and he started out visiting various mediums to make contact with his dearly departed mother, whom he absolutely adored. In the process, he found to his horror that not only could none of them contact his beloved mother, but most were deceitful cheats. His curiosity about the premise of an afterlife soon took a backseat to his passion to expose these charlatans, and he spent a great deal of his time and energy doing so. He even went so far as to make up a code with his wife, Bess: in case either of them died, the survivor would try to contact the other through a valid medium—the key being that the psychic must verify his or her legitimacy by cracking the Houdinis' communication code. In that way, fraud would be ruled out, and the continuation of the soul would be proven to the spouse left on Earth.

Harry Houdini died due to peritonitis from a ruptured appendix in 1926—as fate would have it, on Halloween—and for the next ten years, Bess held annual séances to try to contact him. The famous medium Arthur Ford supposedly broke the code in a séance with Bess, but skeptics say that she'd revealed it to reporters a year before that. Bess was mum on the subject, but she also didn't conduct any more séances after 1936. Nevertheless, Arthur Ford was considered to be one of the best psychics the world ever produced.

Edgar Cayce, however, is probably the world's most renowned medium. Born in 1877, he died in 1945 after having given more than 14,000 readings. During his life he also founded the Association for Research and Enlightenment (ARE) based in Virginia Beach, Virginia, which is still operating today. Cayce was known as the "sleeping prophet" because he'd go into a trance state and give readings to individuals—most of whom were not present.

It's interesting that as I read some of the transcripts of Cayce's readings, I noticed he said, "*We* have the body," indicating a plural usage that suggests at least one spirit guide was helping him, yet, to my knowledge, Cayce never acknowledged one by name. He'd put himself into his self-described sleep, and then he'd reach a higher consciousness in which he could access the "Akashic Records" (the archives of each individual's existence) on the Other Side and gather information from them. He was also known for his ability to heal and prescribe treatments for those who were ill.

It took the ARE more than 25 years to catalog all of Cayce's readings; my church and corporation are still registering and transcribing my own trances on myriad subjects, which is a never-ending task (at least while I'm still alive). I have had the advantage of doing trances strictly for scientific and philosophical investigative purposes on specific subject matters, as most of the sessions are devoted to research and not individual readings. It will be a great legacy to leave to the world when I'm done with this life, and I'm humbled and grateful to Mother and Father God for the opportunity to do so. (Note that both of our Parents make up one God, so when I refer to God, I mean both of Them.)

❄ ❄ ❄

It was only after starting my nonprofit foundation in the early 1970s that I began to fully utilize the trance capabilities of my mediumship; before then, I just tended to do so for my family or good friends. I now see what was holding me back wasn't that I didn't trust my ability or my guides—it was the fact that a new career as a professional psychic and spiritual instructor would require total commitment to it, which I wasn't sure I could give.

Up until that time, my abilities had been purposely confined to the people I was really close to and the occasional student who needed help. I'd been a teacher for many years in the Catholic-school system, educating all grades from kindergarten through senior high school. Starting in Missouri and ending up in California, I was perfectly happy to teach forever because I loved it so much. Then as fate would have it, my life took a completely new direction.

I'd just gone through an acrimonious divorce from my first husband (who was not enchanted by my psychic ability unless it served his own means), when I met one of the great loves of my life. Bob Williams was a professor in my master's program, and after quickly ascertaining that I had psychic ability, he became so enthralled by it that he pushed me into the public eye. He was a great one for surprises, which usually meant he'd tell everyone in his circle of academia and friends that I'd do readings for them— but he'd keep me in the dark about it until the very last minute.

One evening he announced to our class that I'd do readings for them instead of having the usual academic session. Although I was flabbergasted and a little peeved that I hadn't been consulted about this announcement, Bob nonetheless quickly set up an area in the classroom for me to work, sat me down in a chair, and asked, "Who wants to be first?" He exuded such power and charm that he easily got me to do it. As he'd explain to me after these surprises, if he *had* consulted with me beforehand, he would have been met with resistance. He had such faith in my abilities that he'd always say, "Sylvia, you just need a little push in the right direction." In truth, he was right.

It was Bob who really started getting me to use my gift on complete strangers. Now, it's one thing to use your psychic ability with people who know and love you, and quite another to do so with people who don't. It was frightening, especially considering that I didn't feel all that secure in my abilities back then. However, Bob's enthusiasm and support helped alleviate my doubts, and I found myself being pulled along in his well-meaning, hell-bound-for-leather crusade of presenting whom he believed was the next great psychic of the world—me!

Of course, I couldn't help but fall in love with him. There was only one problem: he was gay. I even tried to bridge that chasm by suggesting that platonic marriages do work, but he'd just laugh and say, "I love you deeply, as I know you love me . . . but no." Knowing that our relationship could only be platonic didn't deter me, though, and we continued on with our marvelous friendship for quite a while.

When Bob told me that he was going to Australia on a trip, I got a bad feeling and begged him not to go. He went anyway, and several months later, he contracted a staph infection and died. I went into a period of complete devastation and grief and was so angry, both with myself for not being more insistent that he stay home, and with him for not listening to me (a situation that was to repeat itself later on with another dear friend). I still miss Bob to this day, but my initial sorrow was somewhat alleviated by the fact that I'd found a new love in Dal Brown.

Dal loved me, too—and not in a platonic way! And just like Bob Williams had been, he was very positive about my psychic abilities and encouraged me to finally go public with them. Dal and I got married, formed a nonprofit foundation for psychic research, and opened up a small office in Campbell, California. It was during our first years together that we started recording and transcribing trance sessions for study. Over the years, the accumulation of material on various subjects reached thousands of pages, some of which are now in this book.

About *Psychic Healing*

I've broken this book down into two parts: Part I introduces you to the concept of healing yourself, and it's written solely from my point of view; Part II, on the other hand, comes directly from Francine and Raheim and shares their considerable wisdom as they take the subject further. Part II contains the actual transcripts from research trances (although they've been edited for content and clarity) in which my spirit guides imparted information to various groups over the years; they make up only a small percentage of what we have in our files. Included are various questions on health and healing that were asked by participants, as well as the answers provided by either Francine or Raheim.

Since this work contains quite a few trance transcripts, I do want to give kudos to my guides for their help and support in my life. Francine has told me often that if she isn't well versed on a particular subject, she brings in experts from the Other Side to assist her in offering whatever might be useful. And even though she and I disagree on things now and again (and most times she's right), I truly love and respect her.

The bulk of the transcripts that appear in these pages is in fact from Francine, with Raheim contributing from time to time. I never have conscious memory of trance sessions or what's taken place in them until I either listen to the recording or read the transcript. This has led to some instances in which a trance sitter (one who's a witness to, or participant in, the session) assumes that I know what's transpired. I've come out of trances and been bombarded by clarification questions from well-meaning sitters who don't realize that I have no clue about what just happened—it can be both funny and a little frustrating because I'm always the *last* one to know. It's especially aggravating in research trances because the group will be all excited by something that Francine or Raheim said, and I have to get it secondhand by having somebody tell me what went on.

The knowledge imparted by my guides in these pages is priceless and prescient, especially when you realize that it heretofore hasn't been released to the general public. So, since valuable information that can aid all of us awaits, let's get to it and become further acquainted with the methods of psychic healing.

❧ ❧ ❧   ❧ ❧ ❧

PART I

Healing
101

Chapter 1

Listening to
the Body's Messages

It seems that just about every day I see advertisements from what the medical profession calls "maverick doctors," who are urging me to buy their newsletters or books that detail their unconventional cures (employing vitamins, natural remedies, or other healing methodologies). It seems that these men and women are fed up with conventional, and sometimes unnecessary, methods of treatment that cost too much and are out of date . . . and I can't say that I blame them.

Please don't get me wrong, I love doctors—I work with many of them and fully believe that they're necessary for the well-being of society—but the medical field is hampered by its own bureaucracy and predilection for profit. Almost any physicians worth their salt will admit that health care is so expensive that many people can't afford it.

A lot of folks have been getting affordable medication from other countries, but the American government's involvement is now restricting this practice. Lawmakers are using the excuse that quality control can't be maintained on drugs produced elsewhere, but the real reason is financial. Pharmaceutical manufacturers in the United States have powerful lobbies that "persuade" our legislators to restrict these outside medicines—but if quality control is such a problem, then why aren't Canadians, Europeans, and Latin Americans dying in droves? Do the drug companies in the

USA think that they're the only ones who can make effective medications? Of course not . . . it simply comes down to the almighty dollar.

Although money is the driving force in our society, we should all be focusing on quality of life. I mean, all the cash in the world won't help us if our health is poor. Would we be able to enjoy our wealth if we couldn't get out of bed? Of course not!

Wellness is at the top of the list for quality of life, so make sure that you're in control of your own—open your eyes and ears, and don't let other people dictate what you should do. It's crucial that you find a doctor who's progressive and willing to work with you; when you find this person, be sure to ask a lot of questions, and don't be afraid to get a second or third opinion. No one knows your body like you do, so if something doesn't feel right, search until it does. Keep in mind that you also have to be reasonable and realize that if the cure is worse than the illness, then maybe you should take another look at your options.

Try to go to specialists when you can, because most of them are up-to-date on the newest treatments in their fields. Even though general practitioners (GPs) can be just fine, they simply can't keep up with every new development in so many medical areas. No matter if they're specialists or GPs, though, find those you can talk to and who will listen. They should be open-minded to the point that if they're unfamiliar with an alternative treatment you suggest, they'll at least investigate it.

I told my doctor about a simple test I read about that supposedly could detect cancer. He didn't know about it but was very interested, so on my next visit I brought him a copy of the article to check it out himself. He told me, "I'll be sure to read this, and if it works, it can indeed be a great diagnostic tool." That's why I like him so much—he listens and is genuinely open to anything that might possibly help his patients, even if it's unconventional.

Now, as a practicing psychic, author, lecturer, and spiritual teacher, I've had my inevitable run-ins with people in the medical community. I also have many fans and acquaintances in this community—in fact, this may come as a surprise, but I have many more friends than detractors. I think that one of the reasons this is so is because I recognize the need for medical professionals in society. I may disagree with them from time to time on certain issues or practices, but by and large I respect these people of science more than the average person might because I've worked with so many of them and realize how much the world needs them.

My detractors are entitled to their opinions, but in *my* opinion, they're missing the point. I'm not on this planet to fight with them or take their place in any way . . . I just come from a more spiritual and philosophical viewpoint than they do. But I always try to help humankind in any way I possibly can.

In these pages are proven methods of healing, documented in my case files, which have worked for many. *Yet I want to emphasize that these methods should be performed in conjunction with, and under the supervision of, a medical physician.* I also encourage doctors to study these approaches and allow their patients who want to use them to do so whenever feasible, since they can only augment any traditional treatment that's been given.

The True Power of the Mind

Since thoughts are things, we can choose to make life happy, healthy, and free from stress—and certainly less depressing and tiring. So many people I encounter at my lectures, salons, phone readings, and book signings are more depressed and tired lately than they've ever been. Sure, it's a sign of the times, but thanks to the different techniques I'll be sharing in this book, it will now be much easier to spiritually rise above the things that challenge us and bring us down. Truth and knowledge will always set us free in mind, body, and spirit.

The worst thing we can do is internalize. Keeping things bottled up inside or staying focused on illness keeps us too centered on ourselves and draws negativity to us. It's perfectly natural for the body's parts to give out because of wear and tear as we age, but why not try to stay as well and as active as we can until the end comes? Sure, we all have our complaints, which I know about firsthand. I have a crack in my upper thighbone, thanks to my first husband, Gary, which can't really be repaired because it's not in the hip joint. Some days it's good and some days it's not so good, but I'm convinced that this injury has been a blessing of sorts because it does slow me down a little.

There are so many things our bodies tell us, and usually in a specific and logical manner. Take, for example, what happened to a doctor friend of mine who had saved my life when I was severely ill at the age of 26. Many years later he was dying of stomach cancer, and I went back to my hometown of Kansas City, Missouri, to see him. I asked, "Jim, dear, what is it?" And he said so pointedly, "Sylvia, I just couldn't stomach life anymore." He'd actually transferred all that he couldn't digest in life to his stomach, leaving the door wide open to disease.

Every organ and gland in your body speaks to you quite literally, so if you get sick, the first thing you must do is ask yourself what's going on in your life. How much are you carrying that causes your back to go out? What broke your heart and gave you coronary problems? If you're losing your hearing or your sight, it could be because you've heard or seen too much. And your thyroid can become unbalanced courtesy of too much stress. When I was 12 years old, for instance, I went through a difficult time when my parents were talking about a divorce and each wanted custody of me. After a physical revealed that my thyroid was going haywire, I was put on medication. My parents subsequently worked out the problems in their marriage (later I wished they hadn't), and my thyroid went back to normal. It turns out that the thyroid gland is severely affected by emotion and takes a beating when life pulls us in too many directions.

When we gain weight, this may not just be from overeating, but from issues we faced in a past life as well. (This was the case with one woman I talked to, who'd starved to death in a past life and couldn't get enough food in this one.) Many times, putting on excess pounds is an attempt to combat loneliness; it can also be insulation so that others can't get to us to hurt us. When it comes to those who are too thin or have eating disorders, on the other hand, their mind-set is this: *Everything in my life is out of control, but I can control what I eat! So I can binge and purge because I have power over this one thing.*

As strange as it may seem, it's almost as if we're punishing ourselves for coming into life. Most of us are so homesick for the Other Side that we have this hole of loneliness, regret, and lack of fulfillment, no matter how happy or joyful our lives are. It doesn't matter whether we believe in God and the Other Side, have never heard of that dimension, or just aren't interested . . . that hole is still there, and it causes us a tremendous amount of stress.

In order to fill that hole inside and soothe the onslaught of life, we may turn to substances that poison our body, such as liquor and drugs. For example, my own mother was a prescription-drug addict. She felt it was all right because it was medication that was prescribed for her, although she went to three or four doctors for "help." I think that's why I personally can't stand pills. I do take vitamins, but I have a real aversion to pain pills—and strangely enough, I'm allergic to almost every type of drug. Who knows if I came in with this aversion or developed it as a fail-safe so that I wouldn't abuse substances like my mother did. I'm not trying to say, "I'm so good"; in many ways, this borders on dangerous because I'm allergic to antibiotics and other medications that can really help me if I happen to get sick.

Jesus said that the body is a temple. I feel that we should also look at the body as a new car that we have to take care of and lovingly maintain. If we abuse our car with the wrong type of gasoline or drive it too fast or too hard day after day, we're going to lose that car very quickly. However, if we replace the tires and the spark plugs, get regular oil changes, and keep it clean, the major parts of the engine and transmission will stay intact and last a long time.

It's a statistical fact that the human life span is increasing. Even life-insurance companies are now raising the age of those who qualify, which is a real indicator that people are living longer. However, it's important to make sure that our years have quantity *and* quality.

Take a Look Around

Let's get back to how we get sick . . . or, I should say, "allow ourselves to get sick." When our body speaks to us, we should certainly listen. However, we also must be aware of the people and situations we surround ourselves with, as these can greatly influence our wellness.

Know that you can audit your relationship with a family member, spouse, co-worker, or friend. So if you're around someone who makes you feel uptight, stressed, or not yourself, remove that person from your life. Even if it means that you'll be alone for a while, it will be better for your health, believe me.

When I was with my first husband, who was physically and mentally abusive, I got hepatitis A, trench mouth, strep throat, and mononucleosis; and I had major surgery on top of that. Sure, I was teaching, but I'd done so for four years before we got married and had never been so ill. (As soon as I left Gary, I got better, and I haven't been that sick since, thank God!) The stress of working; having my firstborn, Paul; and not being able to please my husband took its toll. I was always on edge, waiting for the so-called ax to fall.

When Chris, my youngest, came along, Gary started in on our children. Well, that did it—I took the boys and left. I had no money and was forced to live in a tenement, but we were safe and happy. We ate a lot of pork and beans and drove around in a car that only worked sporadically, but the trade-off was worth it—my kids even thrived in school. So whenever people tell me that they can't give up their lifestyle, I want to say (and most of the time do), "Then you'll give up your *life* or you'll become too sick to live." When I left my husband, I did have pneumonia, but I recovered quickly . . . and I'm sure that had I stayed, I wouldn't have lived very long at all.

Before I divorced my husband, I also developed chronic cystitis. My bladder burned constantly, and I had numerous medications prescribed to try to stop it, but nothing worked. One day at a conference I mentioned my problem to a doctor friend of mine. He said, "Well, besides that, what's going on in your life?" I was explaining how I was taking care of my sister and trying to keep peace in my family when I blurted out, "God, my family pisses me off!" As soon as I said it, a lightbulb came on and I exclaimed, "Oh, that's it!" From that day to this, I've never had another problem with my bladder. Sometimes it's so true that we can't see an answer that's right in front of us.

If someone is a pain in your neck, squeezing the life out of you so you can't breathe, breaking your heart, or making your blood boil, get away and find your place of peace. While you have written this in for yourself, the purpose of your chart is to learn from it . . . not wallow in it. Once it becomes apparent that the way you live is making you ill, you need to change it.

If you've charted to have an illness, look at talk-show host Montel Williams for inspiration. He's had multiple sclerosis (MS) for more than 20 years, yet he won't give up. While most people who have had MS that long are in wheelchairs, he keeps himself in peak physical shape and even snowboards. I know that my dear friend is in pain much of the time, but he chooses to ignore it and eats right, exercises, and follows all of the best medical advice that he's garnered and researched from all over the world.

Keep in mind that after learning from your charted illness, you can also ask to be healed. Think of your body as a car that needs repair—fix it and then go on. We all age, but we can do so gracefully with a lot of preventive maintenance. If, let's say, your family is genetically predisposed to heart disease, then you can exercise and watch your diet, blood sugar, blood pressure, and circulation. I find it very sad that too many people just surrender, feeling that they're victims of their genetic makeup.

Conscious vs. Subconscious

The mind is the most powerful tool we have available to us, and when we're hitting on all cylinders, we feel good, we have energy, and we're healthy. Throw a wrench into our lives, however, and we very quickly break down. For example, we all know at least one person whom we'd kindly call depressed . . . although the more accurate term would be *negative*. These are the individuals who constantly complain about everything, claiming that nothing ever goes right in their lives—they hate their jobs, their relationship with their spouse or significant other, the place they live, and so on. One other attribute goes with these folks: usually they are sick quite often or are addicts.

On the other hand, we also know people whom we'd deem positive—we love to be around these individuals, and we feel energized by them. These men and women are rarely in poor health, and when they do come down with something, they get over it quickly. Now, what causes one type of person to be susceptible to illness over another? There can be numerous factors, but one of the biggest is that the subconscious and conscious minds are in harmony with each other in the positive person who rarely gets sick, but they're in *dis*harmony in the negative person who seems to be constantly under the weather.

When most of us become ill, we think it's because we caught some germ that infected us. This may be true to a point; however, we come in contact with so many microorganisms each day of our lives that if they were the only cause, we'd be sick all the time. The human body is a wonderful God-made machine with built-in mechanisms such as antibodies to fight the millions of germs we're exposed to daily, and it usually does a fine job of making these bugs ineffective. When our defense mechanisms *do* fail, it tends to be because our conscious and subconscious minds aren't working together.

It turns out that your subconscious mind knows much more than your conscious mind does. The subconscious mind is like a sponge that sops up everything you've ever encountered in life, as well as everything you've encountered *before and after* life. It's like a huge data bank that stores your entire existence—this includes all of the memories of this life that your conscious mind has forgotten, as well as all of the memories of your prior incarnations that your conscious mind has no awareness of at all.

Since your subconscious mind has all this information and your conscious mind only has a limited perception that pertains to your life now, that's where potential problems lie. When conflict occurs, it's typically because your conscious mind is directing you since it thinks it knows what to do, while the subconscious mind actually *does* know—and they don't agree on the best course of action. As soon as such a disagreement occurs, you'll almost certainly get either a mental or physical reaction that manifests itself within you.

A perfect example of this type of conflict comes from the workaholic. Such an individual's conscious mind (programmed by society) says, "In order to get ahead in this world, I must put in long, hard hours to get promotions and more money to buy things." He may have other influences underscoring this belief, such as a spouse who wants a nicer home, the need to keep up with a successful sibling or friend, or a hard-driving parental figure . . . I could go on and on. The point is that the person starts working more to accomplish the goals of making money, getting promoted, and gaining accolades with titles and so forth. Instead of an average workday, he starts to put in 10, then 12, and even 16 or more hours each day to accomplish what he feels he needs to do. The conscious mind of the workaholic drives him onward to greater glory and monetary stature in life.

Meanwhile, his subconscious mind knows that hard work is fine if done in moderation, but if overdone, eventually his body will start to break down or he'll neglect the important things in life such as family and love. Knowing this, the subconscious mind tries to communicate with the conscious mind that this person should slow down and stop and smell the roses. The conscious mind laughs and says, "No way, I've got to reach my goal!" The subconscious takes the rejection in stride and replies, "Okay, if you won't listen, then I'm going to lower the defense mechanisms of the body. I'll *make* you slow down by getting you sick."

Think of some instances when you became ill. I'd venture a guess that more often than not, they occurred right after you were inordinately stressed out or some trauma happened in your life (such as losing a job or loved one, or going through a divorce). In either case, the subconscious and conscious portions of your mind were most likely in conflict with one another. To take this point even further, think of a time when you were madly in love or infatuated with someone: you couldn't sleep, your energy was boundless, you were happy to the point of being silly, and romantic songs or places sent you soaring like an eagle in the sky. Your body took a beating and your endurance was tested to its limits, but I'll bet you never got sick. This is because your conscious and subconscious minds were in harmony.

You can redirect both of your minds to work together so that you don't have any more conflicts. There are several tools to help you do so, such as hypnosis, meditation, prayer, affirmations, and the like. Yet even if you use these tools, you must still learn to listen to your subconscious mind through dreams, health, energy levels, intuition or hunches, conscience, and feelings; this will help you avert any disagreements with the conscious mind. Hypnosis is a good technique to utilize for programming your mind—hypnotic regression is particularly effective because it's exploratory in nature as well as being a potent healing method. It's imperative that you also work on discarding the garbage you've carried around by letting go of the past . . . which brings us to the topic of the next chapter.

❦ ❦ ❦   ❦ ❦ ❦

Chapter 2

How the Past
Can Heal the Present

I'd like to take a moment to explain what the term *cell memory* means, since I'll be referring to it often in this book. Our bodies are made up of millions of cells, each of which has our genetic code, or DNA, imprinted within it. Cells join together to create form and function, which means that it takes billions of them to make up an arm, a kidney, or any other part of the body.

Every individual has a different genetic code, which makes everyone unique. While no one else has our specific genetic code (which is why DNA is used in forensics), certain aspects of it will show up in our children (which is why DNA is also used for paternity identification).

New and astounding research is being done every day to try to identify the genes (our body's blueprint, so to speak) that not only comprise our makeup, but also dictate our mental and physical health. For instance, people who are afflicted with certain diseases carry genes in a particular sequence that makes them predisposed to those ailments. There's optimism in the scientific community that genes can be "rearranged" to treat disease—or even prevent individuals from being susceptible to it at all.

I'm deviating a bit here, so to cut to the chase: *cell memory* refers to the storage of everything we've been through, throughout our entire existence, which is given to each cell by the subconscious mind. In other words, every cell in our body has retention of this life *and* every incarnation we've had since our creation by God.

If a cell fails to operate correctly, then that creates a corresponding effect on the body or mind. It's natural for cells to age, die, or regenerate themselves; when they work like they're supposed to, we're in a very healthy state of being. It's when they *don't* operate properly that health issues arise—and it's precisely this issue that I'll be addressing in this book, which is meant to help you live a full and healthy life.

The impact of cell memory on the body is highly important when it comes to health. I have so many cases in my files of people contracting an illness due to cell memory that I know for a fact it's not an aberration. (My book *Past Lives, Future Healing* explains this in some detail.)

The Case for Reincarnation

Talking about prior lives, of course, brings up the whole premise of reincarnation. Well, I apologize to those of you who don't believe in the subject, but bear with me and try to put yourself in the mind-set of just accepting the *possibility.* I've put forth proof on the existence of reincarnation before, but this is a good time to visit the subject again. (This will also come in handy for those nonbelievers you're trying to convince at social gatherings.)

First and foremost, there's more evidence for reincarnation than there is against it. In fact, the only arguments skeptics ever make against it are of a philosophical or religious nature. Those of us who believe in reincarnation have much more than that, for we can point out logical statements as well as case histories that certainly bode well in our favor. Let's begin with some good ol' deductive reasoning.

All of us reside on this planet we call Earth, but that's where the similarities end. Some of us live longer than others do; some of us inhabit wealthier countries or safer environments; some of us are richer, while some are poorer; some of us are subjected to discrimination, while some are not; some of us are very religious, while some of us don't adhere to any particular faith; some of us are happy, while some of us are unhappy; some of us are good, while some of us are bad. I could go on and on, but I think you get the point that there's inequity in life!

How, then, do we all get an equal opportunity? Is God so callous that He allows one person to have a hundred blissful years of life, while another gets only a few painful days? Skeptics, especially religious ones, will say that "it's a mystery" (what an argument!) and that "only God knows" the reason for this. Other doubters will say it only proves that God is not merciful; rather, He takes His wrath out on humankind by "allowing" these inequities of life. This perpetuates the fearful and angry God these evangelicals use to control the masses as they convey their bigoted message that the only way to salvation is through their particular teachings—a message they spout to whoever will listen, especially those who might contribute greatly to their coffers so that they can continue to spread that message.

Sadly, thanks to ignorance or fear or their own insecurity, many in this world buy in to these prejudicial "religious" teachings. These particular dogmas don't even make sense, since they feature a God Who should be feared and Who can be wrathful and vengeful, yet in the next breath is called "loving." You can't have it both ways—if God is loving and merciful, then He is not vengeful and wrathful and to be feared! Such doctrines are nothing more than a reflection of imperfect human behavior, and God is certainly *not* imperfect.

Reincarnation isn't actually condemned by any specific religious writings (including the Bible), and it won't compromise any spiritual instruction; perhaps that's why more than two-thirds of the world accepts it in one form or another. Skeptics will point out that this includes the belief in transmigration of the soul (the notion that you come back in another life form such as an animal), but that's relegated to Eastern philosophies—Western philosophies tend to negate this. I personally feel that reincarnation is an enhancement to any faith or school of thought because it's a merciful and loving belief.

Our Creators' love is all-magnanimous and all-encompassing, and it isn't only given to those who are intrinsically good. Christ tried to put this forth in his teachings when he said, "Love your enemies," and even when he warned, "Judge not, lest ye be judged." Taking the concept of Mother and Father God loving all in creation a bit further, then we can logically assume that They love *all* the members of every ethnic, religious, and economic group . . . and on and on it goes. In other words, They love every single person and thing in creation. If They didn't, then They would be imperfect.

So why would our Parents allow inequality among Their creations? I believe that there are two reasons. First, it creates an environment in which negativity can endure, which gives us all a chance to learn for our soul's evolvement. After all, how can we know what's good unless we can compare it to something bad? If everything in life were wonderful, we'd all be in paradise. Those of us who live on this planet know that it is most assuredly not paradise—religions know this, too, since they all have a concept of paradise and none of them say that it's this world.

The other reason that inequities exist is because of humankind's imperfection, which causes an environment for evil to flourish. You might protest, "But Sylvia, then that means God is *allowing* evil to flourish." Yes, They do, but only on this temporal plane we call Earth. Using logic again, Mother and Father God are perfect in Their love and mercy, and They love all of Creation (which even includes what's evil).

Knowing that these inequities exist, rational thought dictates that if we have only one life to live on this planet, it would be totally unfair and illogical for one entity to have more of a chance to learn and live here than another. We must then come to the conclusion that God has provided a level playing field through reincarnation.

Reincarnation can be the only logical explanation for why certain entities get more "breaks" than others do. This way, the "have-nots" can have another life in which they could get those opportunities that weren't available to them in a present life. Trying to simplify it as much as possible, *everyone* gets the chance to experience and gain knowledge in all conditions: everyone can choose to live a long or short life; a healthy or sick one; as a member of a different race or sex; and on and on. The bottom line is that all created beings can, of their own free will, determine any type of life they want to live. Selecting these incarnations is like picking a curriculum for souls to learn for their own perfection. It also allows souls the opportunity to pick things up quickly or slowly according to their own needs, and to even take a course of study over again until they have it right.

How Hypnosis Can Help

I didn't believe in reincarnation at first (actually, I never even thought about it)—I was actually convinced of it many years ago when a client came in for a hypnosis appointment for habit control. We were in the middle of his session when he suddenly began describing building pyramids and lapsed into some kind of language I couldn't understand. I found out later through a professor friend at Stanford that my client was speaking in an ancient Assyrian dialect that was thousands of years old!

This incident had a profound effect on me, and I began to research the subject of reincarnation intensively. I figured that if this client could go into what appeared to be a past time and even speak in a long-forgotten language all of a sudden, then there must be something to it. I further reasoned that if *he* could go into the past while under, then maybe hypnosis would be a good tool to regress others.

My organization has countless files on hypnotic regressions that we've performed on various people from all walks of life and religious beliefs; so many dates, names, and places have been verified that we're certain reincarnation exists. Skeptics will say that the individuals we regressed could have looked up certain dates or facts about historical times. Yes, they could have . . . had they wanted to cheat or create a hoax. I know that of the thousands of men and women I've witnessed under regression, most of what they related could be checked—obviously, they all weren't all cheats, nor were they intending to perpetuate any sort of hoax.

Skeptics have a huge weakness in their logic: they believe that if they can duplicate something through trickery, then that something couldn't possibly be true. They forget that they're the only ones taking this approach; when it comes to those who actually go through hypnotic regression, they don't have the intent to deceive anyone. They're only relating what they see, feel, and remember with their subconscious mind.

Taking the premise that there's at least a real possibility that reincarnation exists, let's address the implications. We human beings are a composite of our own experiences—our likes, dislikes, phobias, beliefs, and so on all stem from them. Yet some of us don't realize that what we've experienced hasn't come just from this life. For example, if we're overprotective parents now, it may be because we lost a child in a past incarnation.

What are some of *your* behavioral patterns that could be the result of challenges you faced in the past? If you don't know, allow your subconscious mind to communicate with you (a good way is through recurring dreams or feelings). It can also be quite helpful to use hypnotic regression, so if it's possible for you to explore your past lives in this way, then by all means, do so. I think you'll find that the extra knowledge you obtain is very useful in explaining some of your behaviors and actions as well as gaining more insight into what makes you tick.

❀ ❀ ❀

Hypnosis puts us in an extremely peaceful state of mind, yet we'll also be in an altered type of consciousness. Depending on the individual, this ranges from predominantly *alpha* brain activity (a light, relaxed state almost like daydreaming) to *theta*—and in rare instances, *delta*—activity (deeper states of altered consciousness like sleep). As we learned in the last chapter, most of us tend to relate to only our conscious mind, so any altered state, and especially hypnosis, will enable us to reach our wiser mind much more readily.

Hypnosis can aid you in finding and facing your phobias to help you better understand your behaviors, which may stem from a former incarnation. For example, you might have an unnatural fear of rejection that causes you to be overly possessive, but you can tell your mind and body that the situation that created the anxiety has already happened and has nothing to do with the life you're in now. So if you have a severe condition such as chronic bronchitis, explore your past lives to find out why this is occurring. You can use this process with almost any behavior pattern that's causing you difficulty; when the reason behind it is discovered, you can change that pattern and become the best person you can possibly be.

Until psychiatrists and psychotherapists realize that not all mental problems stem from our parents, then those of us who suffer from them would benefit from looking to our past-life memories as the cause. Most of us really don't need therapists (or need them only infrequently)—the key to sound mental health is to try to be as positive as possible and assist as many others as we can. In the process, we help ourselves because we feel so great about our good deeds. The next chapter will take an in-depth look at this concept.

❀ ❀ ❀   ❀ ❀ ❀

Chapter 3

The Power of the Will and an Ounce of Prevention

One of the hardest things for some people is to be positive, both in their mental outlook and in life. Those who *are* positive in their thinking usually live longer and are healthier than those who aren't. They also tend to be more well liked than negative individuals are. Look at the men and women around you: out of all of them, whom do you enjoy interacting with? Nine times out of ten, it will be the ones who are upbeat in nature. Who wants to be around individuals who are cynical, depressing, inactive, and down all the time? Most of us want to be around those who are up, who easily laugh, who like to do things, and who are generally entertaining and optimistic about other people and life.

I'm more than 70 years of age, yet folks are constantly asking me how I keep up with my schedule. Every year I do dozens of readings, lectures, and interviews; I make countless appearances on television and radio shows; I'm the CEO of two organizations; I research and then write anywhere from two to four books; I run a household; I interact with friends and family members; and I spend so much time traveling that my frequent-flyer miles are in the hundreds of thousands on several carriers!

Everyone around me says I wear them out, and it's a standing joke at my office that those who help me do so in shifts so that they can keep up with me. I have several editors and secretaries—I like to tease them that there seems to be no stamina in people today!

When I take my family on a trip, they tire easily and some of them seem to be sick a lot . . . oh well, youth is wasted on the young! As Mary Margaret, my friend of more than 60 years, loves to point out, when we were teenagers I'd be saying that we should have a party or do something, while my other pals were flat on their backs, moaning, "*Oh no*, we need to rest!"

During my first marriage, I held two jobs, raised two boys, cooked, took care of the house, and attended night school for my master's degree. And my darling dad used to tell me, "Sylvia, why don't you just tie a broom to your rear end—you're constantly cleaning!" I've always had the ability to do a prodigious amount of work, and thankfully, God gave me a body that has held up fairly well, although lately I don't seem to be able to do as much as I did when I was younger. (Whenever I mention this, everyone around me seems to say the same thing: "Yeah, right!")

How do I do it, you ask? Well, I have an overpowering love for Mother and Father God and Their creations (including all of you!), along with an unwavering drive to help as many folks as I can for Them through my work. Oh, and I guess as my ex-husband Dal used to say, "You have a will that rivals God's!" I do admit to a strong will, and many times it's been my savior. When I've been sick, tired, and worn-out—so much so that my body didn't even want to move at times—my will has never failed to get me through to meet my obligations. Of course, I also happen to be very lucky in that I love what I do, and I've always had fairly good health despite some chronic problems stemming from abuse in my first marriage. The combination of my wellness, strong will, and love for God keeps me going and allows me to do what I do.

Your own will and positive outlook can accomplish wonders. If you have a terminal illness, for instance, they can help make you live longer than anyone's expectations and beat the "death sentence." I've witnessed this type of miracle many times, and in most cases it was because the individuals in question actually willed themselves to live and conquer their illnesses or diseases.

If people can utilize their wills to do that, imagine what *you* can do for your own health. . . .

Is Your Body a Successful Company?

I've always believed that the mind is the key to good health. If you're happy and enjoy life, then you're just going to be healthier than most people are.

Here's an analogy to drive this point home. The subconscious mind is like the CEO of the body's company, while the conscious mind serves as the president. Now, the president may run a company, but he must answer to the CEO—and so it is with the mind. Our conscious mind runs our body when we're active and awake, and we follow its direction. However, the subconscious is the true leader and rules us when we're inactive or asleep, at which point it also communicates its wishes to the conscious mind. It's when the CEO and president disagree that problems can result. If they're so focused on their disagreement that they leave the body unsupervised, illness or disease can run rampant, and everything in the company can start breaking down.

It then follows that to stop the process of illness, you have to help your mind get past the conflict and become focused again. Since the subconscious mind has all of your accumulated knowledge, and the conscious mind has only a portion of that knowledge, you should try to address both of them but place your emphasis on the subconscious. You actually communicate with the subconscious mind all the time through sensory input, but to specifically address a problem, you need to communicate with it directly. If you can't convey your desires in this way, then what you want will never take place.

Any altered state of consciousness will give you a faster track and link to your subconscious, and this direct communication is extremely important because it starts the healing process. You can use methods such as hypnosis (be it with a professional or practiced on yourself), meditation, prayer, and visualization. Conscious links such as affirmations are more difficult, but if you use a lot of repetition and say them out loud for greater sensory input, they can be very effective tools of communication as well.

Depression and Our Cycles

Programming yourself with hypnosis can be extremely effective for helping you achieve ultimate wellness. Now, just what do I mean by programming? For the purposes of this book, the concept means nothing more than communicating with your mind and body in a positive manner. You see, the negativity you're subjected to every day can wear you down and cause you to become depressed and anxious, as well as prone to common ills such as colds, flu, and the like. Programming your mind and body to be at optimal health counteracts this and gives you lots of energy.

Hypnosis or meditation can help with "morphic resonance" (that is, what we've carried over with us from past lives, be it good or bad) and with depression and anxiety. In fact, one of the first things you should do when you're in a depressed or anxious state is direct the cell memory to drop any morphic resonance that's causing this condition. Tell yourself that you've already learned from it, and then you can bring your cell memory from something bad to a time in which you were happy and healthy. This should bring you right out of your despair.

Depression tends to occur when your mind and body get overloaded and can be caused by what's going on in your life as well as what's *not* going on; that is, you either think that you have insurmountable problems and too much to do, or you don't even feel like getting out of bed because you don't have enough to do. If you're suffering from the latter, force yourself to get up—tell your body to move and get something done, and instruct your mind to focus on what you're doing. Do any- and everything you can to keep your mind and body active, and you'll soon find that you don't have time for depression. When the human spirit gets broken, it becomes defeated, so don't let *your* spirit break!

I also want to take a second to talk about anxiety here, which has become a real by-product of the negativity we face in this world. One of the most common ways in which anxiety manifests is in the feeling that you can't breathe and are trapped by something you can't put your finger on, which is extremely frightening. Just know that one of the best ways to relieve an anxiety attack is to immediately engage in some form of physical or mental activity. The faster you're able to focus on something other than the dread and panic, the faster you'll get over it.

❀ ❀ ❀

Getting back to depression, what if you feel that you have too many problems to overcome? Well, here's something else to think about. Many years ago, biofeedback researchers discovered that we all have cycles that affect our body and mind. In other words, we have high and low periods of life; in our low cycle, our physical and mental abilities just don't work as well as they do at other times. We have these cycles daily, weekly, monthly, and yearly; we even cycle for years at a time.

In some of my other books, I've referenced a low cycle known as "the desert period," in which we simply don't know where to go or what to do. It's called a desert period because it's as if no matter where we turn, there's only sand as far as the eye can see . . . and no relief in sight. Yet whether we're in the middle of a desert period or just a low ebb in our day, cycles do exist, and we must strive to conquer, or at least survive, them.

If you're astute enough, you can chart your own cycles— and when you realize what they are, you can start programming yourself to get past them. Begin a journal or record of how you feel and perform at certain times of the day or night; and then work up to how you feel over the week, month, and year. Once you've found your pattern, you can commence programming yourself to

25

function better during the low times—you'll get more done and have more energy, eventually being able to operate much like you do in your high cycles. (Some of you already do this when you use your willpower to overcome the blues.)

For those of you who suffer from low periods of depression, no energy, and the like, start disciplining yourself to surmount these conditions. Enlist your determination and use meditation, which will help you communicate with your mind and body to reenergize yourself and eradicate all feelings of depression and tiredness. If you don't have time to meditate, get in touch with your mind by frequently saying affirmations out loud. Over time, you'll need these tools to get out of depression less often because you'll have programmed yourself not to succumb to these low cycles with such intensity.

A Primer on Programming

It turns out that one of the greatest adversaries we face in life is the programming of society. Our world tells us what to buy, what to wear, what to eat and drink, how to act, and on and on it goes. Some of these messages can be beneficial, but most of them are not. Take, for example, the multitude of advertisements we see or hear for certain medications—the companies behind them are in the business of generating serious money, make no mistake about it. Some people will say that these ads make the general public more alert to possible cures or medicines that can help with our afflictions, but these same individuals should be aware that the ads are actually making us conscious of our body's frailty or the possibility that we'll *get* these maladies . . . it's a form of programming.

The diet industry is just as bad. We see and hear so much stuff about eating right—low carb, high carb, low fat, low trans fat, food that lowers cholesterol, food that lowers the *right* cholesterol— that we're inundated with both subtle and blatant programming that affects how we think and feel. There are hundreds of diets out there, and bookstores devote entire sections to volumes on different nutrition plans, including how to eat, what to eat, and in what quantity. Does anyone really know? How about just stopping ourselves from overeating?

It's amazing how much programming we're subjected to every day, particularly of the negative variety. In fact, everything we read in the newspaper or watch on TV seems to be upsetting—no wonder we now inhabit a world full of depressed people. We as human beings absorb so much darkness on a daily basis, and while a positive outlook on life can help somewhat, that won't eliminate all of it. None of us could possibly deflect it all unless we just completely isolated ourselves from the outside world. Since negativity is a part of life, we must accept that we'll be faced with some form of it as long as we live.

Unfortunately, most of us don't understand that the diet of continual bad news we're being fed not only wreaks havoc with our minds, but our bodies as well. All of this negativity has led to increased amounts of stress, which we in the West have manifested into illness. The big problem is that our doctors tend to deal with symptoms rather than the causes. It's not their fault, though: they've been taught to *treat* illness and disease with medicine and surgery, and very little of their training is devoted to *prevention.*

Preventive medicine is neglected so much because the benefits don't seem to be readily apparent. If you go on a healthy-eating-and-lots-of-exercise plan, for instance, it's easy to see the results in weight loss or lowered blood pressure. Yes, diet and exercise are important for good health, but what about the person who eats well and works out regularly but still becomes ill? I have friends who fall into this category, so what are we missing here? Although we can certainly try to be more spiritual and loving, the most important preventive act may be to give ourselves positive programming.

Programming plays a *huge* part in preventive medicine. While it's hardly ever taught in medical schools and few doctors can give lessons in it, it's perhaps your greatest tool in determining your wellness. It goes beyond health to give you greater happiness all around. Without being overly dramatic, it's probably the greatest weapon you'll ever have to battle negativity and its subsequent effects. Programming goes hand in hand with will and desire—you can desire optimal health and a happy life, but are you utilizing your will to obtain them? I'd bet that in the majority of cases, you're not. And if you pray or ask God for help, don't forget that God helps those who help themselves.

Remember, the mind is the most powerful instrument for exorcising the demons of illness and disease. Keeping your attitude upbeat, negating the pessimistic programming you receive every day, and giving your body and mind positive affirmations all contribute greatly to a better and healthier mind and body. If you keep active, help others for God, stay optimistic, and don't allow boredom to enter into your life, then all of the world's goodness and happiness will enter into your life.

The next chapter will look at the concept of positive programming in detail.

❧ ❧ ❧   ❧ ❧ ❧

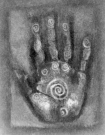

Chapter 4

Program Your Body and Change Your Life

Life is an attitude—so if you have a good attitude, you'll have a good life. As we discussed in the last chapter, a positive outlook will keep you healthier and happier than those who are more negative in nature. Positivity starts with a belief in our Creators and Their love for us, and that belief then blossoms like a flower opening to life and the world. Focus yourself outward with an inward awareness of being, and have faith in your own strength of will and your mind's ability and power.

I cannot stress enough that a positive outlook on life can work wonders for your health, but it can also be enhanced by preventive measures such as affirmations (which are most effective when stated in the present tense). For example, during the flu and cold season, continually tell yourself that you are healthy and that your body fights off any virus that invades it. Just saying something as simple as, "I stay well throughout every season" can be of great help, but do so often and out loud.

But first you must ask yourself if you really want to be healed, or would you rather hang on to your maladies? Remember, your will and desire can make all the difference as far as wellness is concerned, so if you don't have the resolve to be healthy, you won't be. You may have heard about people dying inexplicably from something that wouldn't have normally meant the end of life—that's the will (or lack of it, I should say) at work.

You've probably also heard about folks living far beyond the time they were supposed to pass on. That's because when the will remains steadfast, the body can go on and on, and life can be extended until the point of total breakdown. I know people today who have healed themselves from diseases that were supposed to kill them, and it all stemmed from their will to do so.

This chapter is about using your will and attitude in conjunction with positive programming such as affirmations—the combination of all three is a potent healing force.

Program Your Body for What You Want

Can you spare five minutes or less a day to help achieve your desires? By employing your own God-given tools of a voice and a brain, you can talk to your body and mind and program them to work at their best.

Does this concept sound silly to you? Well, keep in mind that you already do this on a daily basis when you tell yourself, "Damn, I messed up," "Geez, I forgot the bread," or "I have to remember to watch that special on TV tonight." If you learn how to talk to yourself with the premeditated intent to positively program your mind and body, I promise that not only will you start to have better health, but you'll be happier, more loving, and closer to God as well. Negativity won't affect you as it did before, and you'll have a clearer mind and a more fit body. You'll be able to deal with problems easily and make better decisions because you'll be at one with your body and mind, with your will and desire working together instead of fighting each other.

If you have a disease or illness, it's important that you learn everything you can about it—this is especially true as far as the cause is concerned. Then find out the names of the parts of the body that are affected and enlist them in your daily programming. For example, let's say you have diabetes and your pancreas isn't working properly. If you program your body, you can correct the problem by addressing the pancreas and related causes in your own words. (You'd also want to get on a very high-protein diet so that your intake of carbohydrates is low or minimal.)

You must be sure to use your own words in this process. When you do, it becomes easier to instill your feelings so you don't get into the trap of doing something by rote, which cuts down on the impact of what you're saying. And it's crucial that you use as much emotion as you can. If you're angry because you have the disease, for instance, use that rage to fill your words with power. Perhaps you could state something like: "I am in control of my body, and my pancreas works optimally to cure the disease of diabetes!"

Do be sure that you address any illness and organ by name. Also, know what a healthy organ should look like and how it should function; keep in mind that the DNA pattern is there for it to go back to its perfect form, so you can order it to return to optimal health. Visualization is a powerful tool for this—as Dr. Carl Simonton discovered when he told his patients to command the "white knights" (good cells) to destroy the "black knights" (bad cells). Children were his best subjects because they weren't closed off to the idea the way most adults would be.

You can then call on your defense mechanisms and immune system to combat illness and finally program all parts of your body to operate optimally. In addition, if you tell your body that any bad cells currently within it are going to die, it will create an environment that prevents them from reproducing, causing the cells to disappear. Cancer, for instance, is just a bunch of cells that decided to grow without boundaries—if they're allowed to reproduce, they'll displace good, healthy tissue with useless and destructive cells that choke off the function of any organ they invade. They're outlaw cells, but they shouldn't necessarily be feared as fatal; they just grow fast, and the earlier you become aware of them, the better.

Most cancers today are cured or put into remission, but the real key is not to get the disease at all. Yet how can you do this? Maintaining a positive attitude and living a happy lifestyle will keep away 99 percent of common ailments. You can also command your body to produce specific antibodies that fight or just eliminate any renegade cells within it. Get them out of there!

Repeat your powerful words over and over again, for repetition is quite powerful. This programming takes just a few minutes, and you can do it as often as you like during the day. This is very, very effective in helping you cure and combat any disease and in getting your body and mind functioning together to maintain good health.

So when I say that you can talk to your body, I mean it! You can communicate with all of the parts of your physical shell and tell them what you want done by addressing your subconscious with affirmations. Research what your malady is and address the organ, gland, or tissue specifically responsible to make it healthy.

If you feel a swollen lymph gland, for instance, say, "I know you're working hard to protect me, lymph system. I want you to rise up, get strong, go forth, and seek and destroy all causes for this swelling now." Or if you're tired, the primary place to turn your attention to is the pituitary gland, which is the "master gland" that controls all the others. Say, "My pituitary gland is strengthened and energized and put into full, complete functionality and optimal health and vitality. It is cleansed of negativity and darkness."

You can even use programming for skin issues such as cuts and scar tissue. If you cut yourself, speed up the healing process by instructing the lymph cells to flood the area and find and destroy any and all infection. Command the body to immediately cleanse and purify the wound, begin the repair process for every structure that's damaged, reform the skin, and strengthen the underlying connective tissue. For scar tissue—including endometriosis, which is like scar tissue of the uterus—tell it to be replaced by healthy, normal tissue.

Your circulatory system is also very important. The blood can carry toxins, so you want to make sure that your kidneys and liver are functioning properly to filter your blood. All you have to do is instruct your body to produce counteragents called *chelates* so that toxins can be excreted safely. You'll be amazed by how much better you'll feel when you start telling your body and mind to eliminate poisons.

You can utilize programming in other ways, too. For weight loss, let your fat cells know that they won't find a nurturing environment. Direct them to shrink, release their structure, and start dissolving. You can also change your metabolic rate to burn more calories by telling it something like, "Get going! Get off! Just peel off and melt like candle wax, and give me more energy to become more active." (Of course you should also try to get some exercise and eat healthfully and in moderation. I personally prefer high-protein foods, but consuming the right carbohydrates have proven successful for me as well.)

To maintain good health, ask your system to produce every known curative for any invader. Say, "White blood cells, go and find any alien organisms, and destroy those that cause harm to me." Or simply state, "I have optimal wellness! I engage my personal will to be healed and maintain perfect health." And finally, to augment your programming, always make use of all forms of medical help, as necessary.

When You Need to Change Your Entire Life

As we've learned, programming can be very harsh and harmful or it can be a powerful healing tool—society continually sends us detrimental messages, but we can reprogram and heal ourselves effectively to enjoy a full and rich life.

If you're constantly sick, struggling with your weight, dealing with problems that never seem to disappear, or just feeling down in the dumps, you may find that completely changing your lifestyle can make things go away like magic. Your quality of life is so often wrapped up in *how* you live—this can trap you in situations where unhappiness reigns supreme, and your health and well-being will usually suffer shortly thereafter.

Whether you like it or not, your lifestyle does affect your happiness. So take a minute now to ponder the following questions: Are you happy with your work or career? Are you happy with your family and friends? Are you happy with how you've lived your life, or do you feel a lot of guilt and remorse? Are you happy with yourself as a person, and if not, why?

I'm always amazed by the number of men and women who stay in bad situations and endure lives of quiet desperation. It doesn't have to be that way! People will insist that they can't move or change jobs because that's the only security they have in life, and they'll doggedly go through their mundane days in misery. They'll also say that money is the number one factor that keeps them where they are, whether it's because they make so much at their jobs or they don't make enough to free themselves. Balderdash! If you're poor, you can be poor in a different location, and you just might discover more opportunities to become wealthier—or, at the very least, find an environment that's not so depressing or risky.

For example, let's say that a couple lives in a tenement or housing project in a big city because they're poverty-stricken and have a large family. Although both work when they can, jobs are hard to come by, which is at least partially to blame for their situation. The environment is apt to be one in which lawlessness rules and dangerous characters abound—and this couple and their children are subjected to both on a daily basis. It's a surrounding of little hope with poor educational opportunities, drug dealers and pimps in abundance, and dropouts and unemployed people standing around depressed and dejected or burying themselves in addiction or crime. Would you want to live in these conditions? Of course not!

One solution for the couple in question might be to pack up and relocate to a small town or nicer community. The rent of an urban tenement is probably more than that of a modest home or apartment in the Midwest or a rural area. Job security wouldn't be a problem, since these two were only working sporadically before. And planning a move to an area that has employment opportunities doesn't take that much time to investigate if they just put in a little effort. Access to newspapers or the Internet can be found in public libraries, or they could go to an Internet café and rent a computer for a couple of hours to do some research. The point is that it's certainly possible to do the legwork to find a place that has a decent job market.

You might ask, "But what about leaving family and friends behind?" What about it? This couple couldn't make new friends or visit their family members? After all, buses are cheap and go great distances. This would be a small price for them to pay for the chance at greater wealth; a steady job; better schools and a more wholesome environment for their children to grow up in; and, most of all, to get out of the life they're trapped in.

Now what about the folks who make good money but hate their careers or are so stressed out that it's affecting their quality of life? Is it worth it for them to keep things the way they are? Note that the right kind of stress can actually be good because it motivates us, but in Asia people are walking down the street and dropping dead because people must perform over there or it's considered dishonorable. Here in the West, there's certainly no need for stress to drive us to our deathbeds. That's why thousands of people have transformed their lives for the better—if this means a change in profession and a move to another location, so be it as far as they're concerned. They want happiness and will do whatever is necessary to attain it.

It's a big fallacy that wealth equals happiness. I know several individuals who were CEOs of large corporations and abandoned their successful-yet-pressure-packed lifestyles for peace and relative obscurity in the mountains, on a farm, or in a little village. They might start their own small business or live off their savings and investments, or they'll even take a menial job because they love to do it. It doesn't matter to them that they now earn only a fraction of their former salary because they're relaxed, less stressed, and truly content now. The coin flips both ways.

Changing your lifestyle doesn't mean just getting a new job or place of residence, although that can be part of it—it means a complete transformation in attitude about your life and how you're living it. Note that one of the primary causes of disease such as cancer and arthritis is when stress is held within. I know that some of you will say that's ridiculous, but when you evaluate case histories, you'll find that behavior and personality traits are usually shared by those who have these ailments.

For example, these folks tend to be very strong, empathetic individuals who don't want to hurt anybody, so they absorb other people's pain and keep things to themselves. As they try to protect others and create harmony for everyone else, the tension builds within them, and it opens the door for disease. It's much better to find a means for them to release all this pent-up stress so that it doesn't develop into cancer or arthritis—and the best way is a complete lifestyle change.

It's an amazing fact, but people who have cancer and then transform their lives for the better find that the disease either goes into remission or is eliminated altogether. That subject will wrap up the first part of this book . . . just turn the page.

❦ ❦ ❦   ❦ ❦ ❦

Chapter 5

Miracles and the End of Life

I've witnessed plenty of cures and healings in this life that most people would term *miracles*. In the majority of these cases, though, what was at work was in fact passionate will. I'm not saying that actual miracles don't exist, far from it—I've seen those, too, and have had the privilege of knowing that Mother God has intervened many times and caused them to happen. But so many men and women have cured themselves (often with help from the medical community) that I'm convinced it was their own will that did the work . . . they simply refused to give up and die.

I've always maintained that very few of us know the power we contain. If we focus with pure intent and a truly passionate will, there's almost nothing we can't do. It's just like those stories we've all heard in which a diminutive person lifted a car off an accident victim or performed some other miraculous feat in a time of crisis. I've frequently said that if we have the desire, we can regenerate a lost limb, for that's how powerful our minds can be.

As I've repeated so often in this book, you can heal yourself of almost any illness that doesn't go against your chart by engaging your willpower and programming your body and mind. Unfortunately, you may follow these suggestions for a little while but then get tired or bored and stop the programming. Yet what could be more of a priority than your wellness?

Talk to your body over and over again, using positive affirmations and phrases such as "I heal and beat this illness" or "My entire immune system works to rid me of this disease." It's also vitally important to do your programming with feeling. Get angry at having this affliction, and use that anger to give your words power. Don't mess around with being passive—become emotional! Yell and scream if you have to, commanding your body with orders such as "Go in there, cells, and fight off this illness!" "Get off your butt, immune system, and activate and bring yourself to your optimal fighting capability!" "Mind and body, do not give up in fighting off this disease—we *will* be healed!"

The other thing I want to emphasize is the time you must devote to your programming. Yes, a few minutes a day are all you need, but if you can spare more, by all means do so! If you're in the hospital or laid up in bed, what else are you going to do with yourself? Spend as much time as you can meditating and talking to your mind and body, as it will also help you get out of bed and recover more quickly. Keep in mind that programming will never interfere with any other healing methods being done on you, be they conventional or unconventional.

The Happiness Factor

Life here on Earth gives all of us problems in one way or another, which we can't escape unless we become hermits on a mountaintop and just shut out the world. We must deal with life's challenges . . . and it's *how* we deal with them that determines our outlook and the inevitable effect it will have on our health and happiness.

Let's think about happiness itself for a moment—just what is it? Is it having everything we want and need? Is it being independently wealthy? Is it being in love? Is it being active and fit? Is it doing work that we enjoy? Is it having a wonderful family? All of these can certainly be aspects of happiness, and I could list many more.

When we get right down to it, however, isn't it really a frame of mind?

Think about when you were the happiest in your life. You may have been madly in love with someone and working at a job you really liked, with plenty of money to pay the bills and buy whatever you wanted, and everything seemed to be coming up roses. How was your health during this time? How did you look at the world and yourself? Chances are you felt fantastic, both about yourself and life in general.

Think about yourself now . . . are you still that happy? How's your health? Do you have a great and loving relationship? How do you feel about your friends and family? How's your career and financial situation? And most important, how do you feel about yourself and the world? If you're still as blissed-out as ever, then God bless you and yours. Sadly, though, most of us find ourselves in a state where we have moments of joy that are intermingled with moments of pain, seemingly insurmountable problems, grief, despair, and uncharitable thoughts about ourselves and others. Just what causes this? *Life* is the culprit here, and it can wear us down if we let it.

If our outlook isn't positive, we're going to become depressed, ill, unhappy, argumentative, cynical, jealous, lazy, dependent, angry, bitter, peevish, and nitpicky; and soon we'll find ourselves taking out our poor attitude on the folks around us, which just makes the situation worse. When we decide to blame others for our plight and take things out on them, this leads to the breakup of friendships and even families.

The mightiest weapon in the fight against life's adversity is your mind. *In order to be happy and give yourself the power to cure any disease or illness, you must change your mental outlook!* Constantly program yourself to be upbeat, effervescent, and joyful by using positive affirmations and telling your mind and body to be the best person you can possibly be. After that, start doing for others—be it your loved ones, members of a charitable cause, or deserving strangers. The activation of your mind and body will help you feel wonderful, both about other people and yourself.

I promise that if you do so, you won't have the time or inclination to dwell upon your own problems as much, and any negativity will greatly dissipate or even disappear. You'll create a positive aura around you, and you'll learn to love yourself. From this point, ultimate happiness and miraculous healing are easily within your grasp.

Going Home

If you do everything that I've mentioned in these pages so far—consume nutritious foods and beverages, exercise regularly, keep a positive mental outlook, and continually program your body and mind—you're guaranteed to have optimal health. Yet, at some point or another, the inevitable is going to happen: you're going to pass over to the Other Side.

The problem with death is that it causes so much fear in people. But what's behind that fear is actually the lack of knowledge about what happens after we pass. I'm one of the lucky ones because I *know* what happens; and I've tried to convey that to countless people through my books, lectures, and media appearances. I know that unless the heavens part and you can actually see what awaits you after you die, most of you will have a bit of uncertainty when I tell you that you'll be going to a true paradise.

The dread of death and what comes after it is underscored by various world religions. I don't know of one that's refrained from having some sort of negative codicil for "sinners"; frankly, I don't understand how religion can judge people and incessantly preach about how their souls are going to "hell" when it's the individual soul that judges itself. As I've stated before, Mother and Father God are all-merciful and loving, which means that They care about all of creation—including sinners—and would never condemn anyone to a so-called hell (which, of course, doesn't exist).

40

The closest our Parents come to judging anyone is when they keep what are known as "dark entities" from joining the rest of us on the Other Side. These evil souls are then recycled back into life, and they'll continue to be until this particular schematic of reincarnation ends, at which point they'll be reabsorbed back into Them. Nothing is destroyed by God, and nothing in creation is punished forever in a pit of burning fire. It's highly illogical that our Creators would destroy or punish Themselves, especially when negativity and evil are only transient in nature and will eventually pass away into the eons of time as more of Their schematics unfold.

Emphasizing the fear of God and death is one of the biggest travesties of organized religion. The world's faiths are too steeped in the traditions and dogma made centuries ago to change their viewpoints, and humankind must unfortunately suffer for it today. Thankfully, there are rebels out there, and I've always been impressed by their ability to reject what churches have perpetuated and think for themselves. Rebels keep these huge bastions of religion at bay, despite all their money and power. Because they give out light, knowledge, and truth to those who seek it, such individuals are truly God's lampposts.

Getting back to what happens when you pass on, rest assured that you'll be going to the most majestic, magical place you can think of, whether you think you've lived a good life or not. Your soul learns by your own experiences, so when you go Home, you'll judge yourself and decide if you want to come back to do it right the next time.

There is no "Judgment Day" awaiting you—Mother and Father God forgive you for any transgressions because They know that you're human and can err. You'll also see where you erred when you review your life on the Other Side, and then you'll take appropriate action to correct those mistakes. That's the sum total of your "judgment," which is nothing but a learning process to make your soul more spiritual by obtaining additional knowledge through experience. If you need a hundred chances or more to get it right, our Parents will give them to you because They love you so much and you are so dear to Them.

I've often said that death will be your happiest endeavor because you get to go Home. This life on Earth is so fleeting compared to the eons of time spent in the true reality of the Other Side. Even if you live many lives, your true Home is always waiting for you, and your all-loving Mother and Father are eternally with you. And remember that your loved ones who have passed over are ecstatic, for they're in the paradise of the Other Side and don't have to suffer the negativity of Earth anymore. They're anticipating the day when you can join them, and that joyful reunion is something you can absolutely look forward to.

💠 💠 💠

My brief tutorial on self-healing has now come to a close, and I hope you've indeed learned something. But now it's time to turn this book over to my beloved spirit guides, who will impart their remarkable wisdom to help you become a master at psychic healing.

(**Note:** The chapters in Part II alternate between Francine and Raheim, and each chapter indicates who's speaking. And at the end of each chapter, I've included some questions that the research groups have posed to my guides, along with their answers.)

💠 💠 💠 💠 💠 💠

PART II

The Spirit Guides'
Master Class

Chapter 6

Passion, Vehemence, and Healing

Raheim: I know you've heard this before, but I want you to really comprehend it: *anyone can heal!* It's not an appointment from God; it's a freely given ability. Naturally, there are some people who have more confidence in their ability, so it will come in stronger with them. But please get rid of the notion that you must be told by any living person that you can or cannot heal . . . because you can. As Sylvia always says, the operative word here isn't *can* or *may*—it's *should*. In other words, not only can everyone heal, but everyone should.

You can also heal yourself! Of course, if you are suffering from a disease or are in a great deal of pain, then you ought to consult with a physician. But you can learn to put yourself in a state in which you can alleviate the discomfort, very much like you have in your world with the controlled breathing of Lamaze. You can also utilize meditation or lay hands upon yourself, a practice that's as old as time.

The correct way to lay hands on yourself or somebody else varies depending upon what your gender is (or what you wish it was or you feel you truly are). If you're a female, place your left hand directly on the affected area and cover it with your right hand. If you're a male, do just the opposite: put your right hand on the area and cover it with your left.

45

If, however, you're a female who's more in touch with the masculine side of yourself, then I'd recommend that you use your right hand first (and if you're a male who feels your feminine side more, use your left hand first). It has nothing to do with your sexuality and everything to do with whether you feel that your masculine or feminine side is stronger. I'd advise you to try your hands both ways to see which one brings you the most energy. Have the person you're laying hands on help you out by saying, "I felt the energy more strongly the first time [or the second time] you did it." This only takes a few moments and can give you insight into which hand is stronger.

You can lay hands on any part of your body—be it your chest, your abdominal area, your back, or any other area. You can also have someone else put their hands over yours, which will enhance the overall effect, or have them lay hands on your hard-to-reach spots. Realize that this healing technique gets its power from God and Their emissaries, such as angels. You can also actually pull Father God's sustaining energy from the atmosphere to channel through you to the person who needs healing, whether it's yourself or someone else. You can direct your own energy, but it isn't nearly as effective as just giving yourself up to become a tube or conduit for God's outside energy.

Sometimes in observance, I see healings that go on too long. When you turn on a faucet, it doesn't tend to trickle; it pours. So don't stand there and only expect a trickle—really open up that tap and let the power pour through you. But don't do a long procedure in which you have people sit for 20 or 30 minutes while you work on them. The first few minutes is when the rapid healing occurs, and if you go beyond five minutes, then you've probably lost the individuals. They'll become very agitated and uncomfortable if they have to sit for that length of time.

Ancient Methods, Modern Cures

As medicine has progressed through the ages, and as so-called civilization has brought new insights into healing methods, an interesting phenomenon has taken place. In this "enlightened" age, certain cultures are still adhering to the remedies practiced by their ancestors. Asian medicine is perhaps the best-known example of this, but many of what you call "primitive" tribes—such as the Inuit, Polynesian, Native American, and even Celtic cultures—have kept within their structure ancient techniques that they know can cure.

Now, as far as healing is concerned, there are no primitive tribes . . . unless you want to talk about North Americans, who are certainly primitive when it comes to intelligence. I say this knowing that the continent probably has the finest doctors, hospitals, and medical equipment on the planet; but they're more ensconced in traditional Western medicine than anywhere else in the world. The ancient modes of healing employed by shamans and herbalists, on the other hand, have given rise to the movement of holism or holistic medicine, which is nothing more than treating the whole person rather than just the symptoms of illness or disease.

Lots of modern-day holistic practices also stem from Wicca, a goddess-based religion that has deep roots in the earth and the natural order of things. It's believed that Wicca can be traced back centuries before Christianity to the old Celtic religions practiced by the Druids, but many followers today say that it's a fairly new religion that has little in common with the ancient devotees.

Wiccans were Earth's original healers; unfortunately, early Christians viewed their cures as works of the devil and branded them as witches or warlocks. People today still tend to confuse Wicca with witchcraft, or they think that it's a sinister practice devoted to "the black arts." Since my avocation on the Other Side is the study of magic, I can tell you that true followers of Wicca aren't evil at all; rather, they have a beautiful religion steeped in Mother God and nature. Their use of herbs in healing has contributed greatly to the movement of herbalism today.

In fact, many cures that bygone generations swore by are now being studied more closely to see if they have genuine healing properties. Take chicken soup, for example. It turns out that this old standby has an enzyme in it that not only helps relieve symptoms of the common cold or flu, it can cure everything from dysentery to dyspepsia—especially if it's cooked with the bone of the chicken and simmered for a long time. Similarly, mother's milk is being experimentally used in the treatment of certain types of cancer.

No one has ever discerned the fact that cancer is viral. Medicine has professed profusely that it's systemic, but I'm here to tell you that it's only systemic in the aspect that you can lower your immune system to the point that you'll get it. Every single one of you who's reached the age of 40 has had, at any given time, minor strokes, all types of arrythmia, heart palpations, and possible ulcerations of the colon; and you've also produced cancer cells. What happens is that your body's antibodies attack these and tend to prevent you from getting any serious illness or disease. If you do become sick, it's probably because your natural immune system was lowered to the point that your antibodies couldn't battle and eliminate the ailment sufficiently.

❧ ❧ ❧

One of the ways to bolster your own natural immune system is to stay away from certain types of stress. However, you on Earth are so worried about stress that you're stressing about stressing! That's why it's important to determine which types are bad and which are good. The strain of taking care of a loved one, for instance, can be an irritation, an aggravation, or a painful process; but because it's done with love, it's not a bad type of stress that will kill you.

Even if you're frantically running around all the time to try to get things done and worrying about your job, bank account, marriage, or children, you're not dealing with bad stress. You see, while everyday living can be stressful, it won't kill you . . . strangely enough, it's the stress of nothingness that does it.

The worst stress that can ever be perpetuated upon human beings is boredom or malaise—the sense that you've given up, you lack any passion, you no longer look forward to what's going to come next, and you don't even want to get out of bed. Everyone goes through periods where they wonder, *What am I doing? Why am I here?* I've done it in my lives, and you'll do it in yours. Yet when it goes on year after year, the will breaks. When this happens, we on my side see the body's antibodies weaken; nothing fights anymore because the will is the ruler of the whole domain of the body.

You might say, "But I've been depressed, agitated, and irritated; I've had nightmares; I'm phobic and I'm obsessive!" Well, that won't kill you! What takes the life out of you is no longer having any obsessions, fears, or purpose in life; it's what we call "the flatline." Guess what happens when you die? You flatline, and that's what can happen if you're still alive.

People may tell you how tired you look, how much you're overdoing it, how much they don't envy all you're going through—don't let those notions plant themselves in your brain! I'm here to tell you that when it comes to spreading negativity, some of the worst offenders can be found in the medical profession. I'm not knocking these individuals because you must go and see them if you're ill, but if they tell you that something is horribly wrong with you, you don't have to accept that. It's like Sylvia has said so many times, "Take control of your life. Take control back to you."

Rev Up Your Passion!

If I were to tell you that you had a finite amount of time left to live, wouldn't you want to do so with activity and passion rather than with malaise and boredom? Even if your days were always frenzied, wouldn't it be better to live with that frenzy than with nothingness? You're at least doing something with your mind . . . if your mind no longer cares and then goes into a flat level of total, abysmal depression, that's when the killer can strike.

It's not just a theory but a fact that if you have no purpose in life, aren't active with your mind and body, and have no passion, then your body is left wide open for disease and illness. I know that you've been told that if you hate others or have anger, you'll get cancer. If you suppress your feelings, that can be true. But I must also remind you that Jesus said to hate wrongdoing and evil. The so-called Christian philosophy—never get angry, don't subject yourself to hatred, always be passive—is controlling. When you're controlled, it's much easier to herd you around; but if you are full of ideas and are a free thinker, you'll chafe at that idea. You may be led by others or want knowledge, but you won't want to be controlled. You'll want to work on your own spiritual journey, which is the most passionate way to live.

I'm not particularly fond of the fundamentalist realm of Christianity, but I have to give them credit for how strong they feel about "the devil." At least they're giving their followers some passion to always be fighting that evil demon that stands in the corner with its pitchfork.

Over here on my side, we've found over all the centuries that people love to be scared for some reason. It seems that when you're frightened, your adrenal glands throw out a great deal of endorphins, and you get rid of a lot of your "stuff." That's why some people like horror movies—they can scream and throw themselves around. They may say, "I can't look," yet they do, and it can give them a type of catharsis. That's why Halloween has always been so popular . . . do you remember what it was like to be a child and see the haunted house and the ghosts and goblins?

Some people may get their catharsis from extreme physical activity, such as bungee jumping, skydiving, or rock climbing; others get it by subjecting themselves to the fear of financial ruin or rejection in love; and still others enjoy roller coasters or other fast and dangerous rides. Human beings, by and large, love to be frightened, so it doesn't hurt to give in to it every now and again.

Don't scare yourself, but at least get excited about *something* in life. Do something that's maybe so out of character that you get your endorphins moving. Your lives on Earth are too placid, so try to do something that is different or has a little risk to it. Go to a restaurant and eat alone—even as small as that is, it's an adventure. Remember that the mundaneness of life is what can just throw you.

I also believe that everyone should keep a journal and jot down their feelings in it. Now I know that not everyone is a writer, but you'd be surprised at what it can do for you. If you keep a daily or weekly or even monthly journal about your life and then periodically read through it, you'll be surprised by the kinds of insights you can get about your life and what's going on around you, as well as what you may need to change or try.

This will be a great legacy to leave to your children or grandchildren, for they can read about you in great detail and get more insight into you as a person—you may even be able to help them with their problems because they can see how you solved yours. You might say, "Oh, it's too personal." Believe me, you've never written or felt anything that your forebears haven't done or thought of, too. You may think you've come upon a new idea, but there's nothing new under this sun—and I'm sure there's nothing new under *any* sun. It's almost a certainty that another human being already thought this, and may even have carried it out with more exquisite sinfulness than you could ever imagine.

§ § §

Getting back to healing, you can reverse almost anything at any point by the will or judgment center. I don't care how close someone is to death—even if the body has caved in or gone into renal failure—if the will is engaged, that person will still live. Yet be very careful that you're not overriding someone else's will; it's not that it's bad if you do, but you wouldn't want him or her to hold on just because you don't want to say good-bye.

Let's talk about chemotherapy and radiation therapy. On my side, we find that these treatments are somewhat barbaric. It's not that we're totally against them, but we do find them to be terribly

51

inhumane, and it seems that there's no dignity in dying anymore. People on these types of treatments lose their hair, become weak, drop a lot of weight, lose the life sheen in their skin, and go through tremendous pain and suffering. This is a case of the cure sometimes being worse than the disease. I'm not trying to influence anyone in any way, but I don't believe in these methods. I realize that some individuals are cured with them, but I feel that there are better alternatives.

If you're deciding whether or not to use these therapies, I'm not trying to dissuade you. I'm just telling you what we see over here, and I want you to be completely informed before you make your decision. Look at everything objectively and through righteous eyes, as a person with logic would. Sylvia is very, very predisposed to Western medicine, but even she has never been for chemotherapy or radiation because they destroy all the antibodies in the body. If you talk to any physician who's honest, he or she will tell you it's poison.

❦ ❦ ❦

Research Group Q & A

Q: Exactly what is chemotherapy?

A: It's a chemical substance that goes through the body, containing reagents that are supposed to kill cancer cells. What it does is weaken the system so that the body has no defenses anymore—the chemicals that are used kill good cells as well as the cancer cells, so the body must fight both the chemicals and the disease. If it were something that was laced with, let's say, a rejuvenator of cells, maybe it wouldn't be so devastating, but it isn't.

Q: What about radiation therapy?

A: This is a treatment in which selective doses of radiation are put into tumors to kill off the cancerous cells. It has many of the same by-products of chemotherapy with respect to the loss of hair, weight, energy, and so forth. You must realize that both chemotherapy and radiation therapy are poisons—although they're being used to kill off cancer-infected cells and growths, any poison affects the body adversely.

Q: Are macrobiotic diets good for people with terminal illnesses?

A: There was a woman Sylvia talked to who had cancer all through her intestinal tract. The doctor said, "We're going to have to do a complete colostomy," which is the way it goes in medicine. Of course, once there's a colostomy bag, everything else goes unattended, and the next place the cancer hits is the liver and then the lungs and then the brain. (Did you know that if cancer starts in the brain, it usually doesn't go anyplace else? It's amazing.)

The woman told the doctor, "Get away from me," and walked out of the office. She proceeded to go on a macrobiotic diet—juicing, lots of fruits and herbs— but she kept her protein count up as well with fish, crustaceans, and amino acids. She saw that doctor after five years of perfect health, and he said, "Well, it was probably a misdiagnosis." Then there was the physician who was diagnosed with cancer by six other medical professionals. This man had it totally throughout his spine (what they call "metastasized"), yet he was also told he'd been given a misdiagnosis when the disease disappeared after he went on a macrobiotic diet.

Asia has it over Western medicine in many ways; for instance, they believe in the power of eating certain foods, and they don't tell their patients that they're dying of cancer. Thus, they have a higher cure rate for this disease than we do in North America.

Q: You say that cancer is a virus?

A: Yes, and the virus that causes it is actually an offshoot of the common cold. Now, if you get a cold, you aren't going to get cancer—this is just a very tiny, virulent form of it. And while there is no cure for the common cold, we know that if your resistance is low, you're going to catch it or the flu.

Q: So should we get vaccinations against the flu and other illnesses?

A: I see no real reason not to. All vaccines have antibodies that have been proven to fight the illness for which the vaccines were made. Not all of them will necessarily be that effective, however, because illnesses are becoming more and more sophisticated. In my last life in India, we used to try to get ourselves infected at a young age with any type of malady so that our bodies could then fight it. It seems like a drastic solution, but we'd do this because medicine wasn't very advanced, and the bulk of the population was very poor and could not afford treatment. Today, many doctors are divided as to whether children should get chicken pox or get the vaccine. But it's the same thing: you subject your body to the illness so that you become insulated and "immune" to it later on.

The strange thing about this is that we often see doctors take all types of antibiotics and everything else to keep themselves from contracting illnesses . . . but they don't prescribe them for you. That's partially because physicians are starting to realize that antibiotics are becoming more and more ineffective. When you take them for every little sniffle or fever, viruses just become more sophisticated and mutate. Therein lies the danger in using a lot of antibiotics: many diseases are becoming stronger and developing a resistance to them.

Some mutant forms of common illnesses are now becoming more dangerous, and the medical community is concerned. That's what's so worrisome about your AIDS virus—it not only hides, but it also converts itself to act like all the other cells. This is a sentient, thinking enemy!

The key to good health is to keep your immune system powerful and highly trained. You can do this by not allowing negative programming to bring your defenses down, and by fighting any illness with passion and vehemence. Say *"No!"* to illness, and mean it! This way, you'll enact your will to control the situation and heal yourself. The more emotion it has behind it, the stronger your will becomes.

Q: How do we help others activate their will and have the passion to heal themselves?

A: You said the word: *passion.* Convince others that they need to have passion to heal and enjoy optimal wellness in mind, body, and spirit. Make them realize that they can actually tell pain and illness to go away with the vehemence and conviction that they're not going to allow it. Tell them to get angry at the disease— how *dare* it try to bring them down!

You bring your whole arsenal of weapons to bear when you call on Father and Mother God, as well as the God within, to create the necessary changes in cell structure to defeat the illness or disease. So if you're doing a healing on someone, call on the will of God. If you do a laying on of hands, make sure that they're in the correct position, open yourself up to be a tube or conduit for God's power, and proclaim, "By the will of God, I am a conduit for healing energy. The God within and the God without are now in the process of changing your cells, and you will be healed!"

Calling on the will of God is very powerful. This is how evangelists sometimes heal people—they scream out that God will heal, and people get riled up to such a high degree of almost frothing excitement that their bodies' chemistry changes. (Understand that the chemistry of the body can actually change quite often, be it thanks to fear, experiencing new things, diet, or movement.)

It sounds very evangelical, but it's so true that if you use the words, you will heal and be healed! Use any words you like, but do so with vehemence and passion because you're programming the mind and body of the recipient. You don't need the loud music, dancing, thumping, and screaming of the evangelist—you can just use the strength and will of quiet serenity, as Jesus did. He never bounced around and screamed; in fact, there's no mention in the Bible or any other religious writings of his acting like anything but a genteel man.

Q: What if you can't always muster up the vehemence to heal?

A: Well, I think it's so important that you train yourself on its use. If you're confused about what vehemence really is, know that it's simply the combination of emotion, passion, belief, and knowledge. Summoning it up is very much like when you notice people grunting or screaming as they do karate. This is a very ancient thing, for it brings about power and focus.

You'd have a hard time being vehement about something you didn't believe in or care about. If you want to be a healer, for instance, your need to help people is a higher calling that will stir up your passion. But if you just want to heal yourself, that's okay—your desire and will to be healed should be enough to bring out vehemence. You can also call other emotions into play, such as anger, to help stir up your passionate side to the point that you could move a mountain if necessary. Only the person who wants to be sick won't be able to bring out true vehemence . . . they'll just mouth words with no passion or emotion behind them, like saying a prayer or the Pledge of Allegiance by rote.

Q: Will this help with programming, too?

A: Absolutely. Since programming helps bolster your healing, it should be done with powerful emotion. The optimal word to use with vehemence is *no:* "*No!* I won't get cancer!" or "*No!* I won't get heart trouble!" Take the words *hope* and *believe* out of your vocabulary. You don't hope or believe you will be healed, you *know* you *will* be healed!

Practice by saying, *"No!"* When you do, you may be surprised to find that all of a sudden, you become flushed, your pulse begins to race, and your heartbeat speeds up. Just by screaming out that *"No!"* your entire body chemistry goes into an adrenaline rush. I know that at first it might be a little bit of a contrivance, but then you'll get into it. It's like acting . . . when Life, the teacher, tells you, "Get up, and do it again!" that's your motivation!

If a parent has died, you're going to have tears and some anger. Your children need you . . . your spouse needs you . . . whatever. You've got motivation now; you're emoting. The more you emote and let your feelings carry the day—versus the body just reacting with the intellect intact—the more success you'll have in your healing. Push the intellect a little bit to the side and then invoke your pent-up emotion.

Q: Will I really feel it in my body?

A: That's right. You don't have to be loud, but do put your hands up and make fists when you proclaim your *"No!"* Do it with so much feeling that you shake—the emotion you bring should make you feel like you have a fever. In the same way, saying, *"Yes!"* brings about an affirmation of power. How many times have coaches shouted, "Come on, winners, let's go!" and the team went out and won? Or then there's the general who stands in front of his army and screams, "We can do it!

Let's all go and win this battle!" He gets those soldiers' adrenaline pumping, and they're fired up to fight hard and triumph.

Adrenaline is good, but most of you on Earth don't use it in the right way. You dispense this golden liquid through your body as a result of things that aren't important. You get your adrenaline pumping because you're afraid that somebody you don't want to talk to is going to call and other silly things like that.

Tell your adrenal area, "Wait and be watchful so that you can give me a great spurt of energy." You can also ask for your adrenaline to go to any area of your body as you affirm: "I am well, I am healthy, and I am free of all illness and disease! I am a strong, living, total entity; and I do not permit any disease or illness to enter my body!"

Thanks to the energy of your vehemence, you won't need a lot of herbs, vitamins, or all of this other so-called healing stuff. Vehemence is cheap, yet the knowledge that you have the power to contradict any negative force in your life—even that of other people against you—is priceless. Remember that while you can put up a shield of white light to protect yourself from others, you've got to have the passion to do so.

Q: Is it easy to call upon vehemence and have our will engaged?

A: Yes, but it must be *real* vehemence—you have to have passion in what you say, and you have to mean it. Here's a thing to do that you'll find terribly fascinating.

Imagine that you have an unruly child or work with someone who's a mess. You can catch their eye for a few minutes, and in your mind, say, *No! You won't get to me or harm me; you won't attack or hurt me. Your negativity can't get to me—it can't surround or target me—I'll neutralize what you're sending to me!* You'll be amazed by the results.

You don't have to stand in front of them and say *"No!"* because that looks too crazy . . . in fact, you don't have to utter a single word. It can be your secret that you're learning to protect yourself mentally using vehemence and passion.

You can also use your passion to send someone healing energy by thinking: *God, make them well! God, help them! My energy and my cellular structure will go and aid them! My cells will travel through time and space to heal their wounds!*

Q: Vehemence works with cells and morphic resonance?

A: Oh yes. It's the old warrior resonance that you've all come for. Did you ever notice that you rarely ever hear about anybody who's in the thick of a battle or doing something that's extremely fun (and even a little bit hazardous) getting sick? They say that an army moves on its stomach and, of course, it doesn't move without food in it. But if you talk to anyone who's ever been in a fight, nothing hurts them because of the adrenaline.

It's very much as Sylvia was remarking to Iena [Francine's name on the Other Side and what Raheim always calls her] recently about a girl who was bitten by a hyena in Kenya. Sylvia was so interested because the girl said that she never felt a thing, and she wanted to return to the beautiful continent of Africa very soon.

Similarly, people who have been in a shark attack say that they noticed the blood before they felt the pain. That's what's so amazing about the body: if you cut yourself and don't notice it, it's only when you see yourself bleeding that you exclaim, "Ouch, I'm hurt!"

Do you realize that it takes almost two-and-a-half seconds for pain to reach the brain? Even though that sounds like a very small amount of time, you can get in a lot of *"No!"* in two-and-a-half seconds. If you see the cut and say, *"No! No! No!"* the healing is much faster.

Also, when you're going through surgery, the very moment that you're under the knife, take yourself to a week or ten days beyond that period and call upon that cell memory in the future. Cell memory goes backward and forward, and seeing yourself well and recuperated in the future aids the healing process.

Q: Can I *"No!"* myself out of surgery altogether?

A: Yes, but be careful. If you need surgery to remove or correct something, then you must do so. But what you can do is *"Yes!"* yourself into wellness and recuperation. I think it's very silly for a woman who has all kinds of tumors that are really affecting her (such as fibroid tumors) to ignore them. There's a point where you've got to take care of it. What I'm trying to do is make you well and keep you that way, since life can easily wear you down. It's like having a big abscess on your neck—

you can *"No!"* it to death, but sometimes you just have to have it lanced.

Q: What about your own healing ability, Raheim?

A: I'm a great healer. I did a lot of it in my last life and have done a bit while in Sylvia's body in trance. I gain nothing from doing these healings except the gratification of seeing a person well and, of course, to brag when I go back and tell everybody that I did it—and I do that profusely, I might add.

All joking aside, it's important that you keep your ego in check when you heal. You can certainly be very proud of the work you've done, but at the moment of healing, be sure to affirm: *I am nothing more than a hallowed vessel. My motive is so pure that all I am concerned about is effecting a healing. I have no other motive except that.* That will put your heart in charge and give you a pure motive.

I think you should keep a record: *this one I healed; this one I didn't; this one I did pretty well; this one I did great.* After all, doctors keep charts, and no one's more egocentric than they are. Yet the only ego gratification for you should be that you were able to be a part of the healing process.

❀ ❀ ❀   ❀ ❀ ❀

Chapter 7

Addressing the Glands and Integrating Different Kinds of Treatment

Francine: To start a healing or program yourself for better health, I'd begin by addressing your glands. This is what the ancient Asians did: they always used the glandular centers in healing by either using needles (that is, acupuncture) or some stimulant to cleanse them. Since your glands are the openings of the body, they'll immediately respond whenever your health is in jeopardy. Be it the thyroid, pineal, or pituitary gland, it will send out a warning to you right away.

Whenever you heal people, you must get them to activate their own glandular system. You don't have to become technical when you do this; rather, just ask, "Is your glandular system in concert with this healing?" Even if they don't know what you're saying, speaking the words *glandular system* will talk to their mind and neurological system to gain access to the glands. Involving the individuals' endocrine system, which is in charge of hormones, will help you create healings that are 99 percent more effective than normal.

Think about it: The pancreatic area provides the body with stamina; if this gets too out of whack, you can get diabetes. The thyroid gland is the motor mechanism of the body; if it goes off, you can develop all kinds of lymphatic problems such as no energy, extreme fluctuations in body temperature, heart palpitations, and hypersensitivity to anything that people say to you. And on and on it goes. . . .

Women have always been told that they're hormonal beings, but they're not the only ones. While men may not have ovaries, this doesn't mean that they're free from hormonal fluctuations. No, males don't menstruate, but they are subject to a type of PMS every month. Any woman who lives with a man will tell you that there's a certain time of the month in which he's off kilter. And we do know that men go through a form of menopause.

Your master gland (the pituitary) is what also creates the aging process because of the dispelling of a certain amount of hormones that you have through your lifetime. When that supply is depleted, the aging process begins. The pituitary gland essentially announces: "This body is now getting ready to die. We must start the aging process and shut down hormones." This makes the hair turn gray and the collagen in the face go away, which causes wrinkling. Then the body's organs begin to slump and sag inside—this isn't just gravity at work but rather because hormones have shut down.

Just like everything in your body, your pituitary gland is sentient and has knowledge, so you can speak to it. Talking to the "central promoter" can be one of your most effective resources, so tell your pituitary gland that you're not aging!

I know that many of you think aging comes down to genetics, but it's actually responsible for only one-third of the equation . . . so you can see how much it comes down to programming. It's like Sylvia has often pointed out: people continually say, "Of course I'm going to get arthritis—my mother did. Of course I'm prone to heart attacks—my father was." What they're doing is telling their cells that they're expecting this to happen, and sure enough, the cells will go along with what's being said.

Arthritic problems are actually the result of trapped energy. Yet even when people who keep everything bottled up inside and can't release their energy show arthritic symptoms, they can still be helped by directing programming to their cells.

Using Traditional and Alternative Treatments

Sylvia was talking to a reputable orthopedic doctor she knows, and he told her, "The one thing you always want to give a patient is hope." When his patients ask this man how long they're going to live, he'll say, "You can live as long as you wish to." The average age that most of you on Earth will reach is around 90 years old—but, as this famous doctor said, hope is strong medicine because it's positive programming.

Of course, programming can be positive *or* negative. While astute family members who urged their loved ones in a coma to wake up have witnessed the impact of their appeals, doctors have been slower to discover the effect words can have on unconscious individuals. It seems that when surgeons have talked about how horrible things were going in the operating room (OR), the subconscious mind of the person being worked on tended to hear and then act upon it. Studies found that eliminating negative talk about patients in surgery cut down on inexplicable deaths in the OR and also aided in speedier recoveries; thus, surgeons now try to keep things positive as they work.

I want to be clear here that I'm not against conventional medicine. It's very much like Sylvia likes to say, "I guess for being a psychic and spiritual person, I'm very unorthodox in the fact that I do believe in Western medicine." Because of this, she's got a great following of doctors that work with her. So if you have a bad heart, you should go and get it fixed—and it's certainly best to start programming *before* any damage occurs. But you can also use it to go through any surgery with flying colors, recuperate faster, and then state with conviction that you aren't going to get into that bind again. Be sure to use visualization when you do your programming because it hits more of the sensory input and makes the technique stronger.

Think of how miraculous it is that the human body knows when it has an infection. Cells talk to cells—we can actually see them nudge each other and run together to go to a wound. It's really phenomenal that these tiny cells know they're supposed to rush as an army to the affected area. If you ever get an infection, you can help the healing process by saying, "I want lymph fluid to come immediately; I want white blood cells to come in great abundance to fight the infection. I want my mind to see that there isn't a cut there at all."

Not that we'd ever do a study by cutting anyone, but if we were to cut a group of people who knew how to talk to their body and a group who had no knowledge of this at all, I guarantee that the people who talked to their body would be on the mend much faster. This one little technique can also enhance wellness altogether.

Don't negate conventional medicine in any way, but be sure to use your mind to enhance it and speed the healing process. For example, when it comes to cancer, people nowadays have multiple methods of care, depending upon the severity of the disease and the wishes of the individual who has it. So let's say that one woman with breast cancer (we'll call her "Patient A") goes through all of the traditional treatments: the lumpectomy or the radical mastectomy, the chemo and the radiation. Another woman suffering from the disease ("Patient B") has done this as well, but she's augmented it with alternative methods. What do you suppose the results will be for both of them?

Just a few years ago, a cancer diagnosis was almost like an automatic death sentence. While this is no longer the case, the public still has the idea that if you get cancer, you're going to die. This is the programming that was hammered into everybody for years, and it's hard to escape that influence. If you do receive a cancer diagnosis these days, you know where you stand and then can take charge and be the captain of your ship.

Most doctors agree that the key to healing depends in large part on the outlook and desires of the patient. So, getting back to our two ladies with breast cancer, if Patient A feels better with traditional medicine, she should continue with it; likewise, if Patient B feels better with her alternative methods, she should keep following them. Both women are comfortable with the treatment they're receiving—and no doctor should talk either of them into doing something they don't want to do. The key here is the patient's attitude and trust: Patient A had no problem trusting in conventional medicine and will most likely beat the cancer. Patient B felt more comfortable supplementing her treatment with alternative forms of healing, but can she also beat the disease? Statistics say she can . . . and she has an even greater chance if she uses her mind and will to further strengthen her plan.

Conventional medicine is full of great healing tools, but there are also many wonderful alternative treatments out there that are very successful. So if you do happen to get seriously ill, explore all of the methods available—both conventional and alternative—to find what you feel most comfortable with, and then use your mind to augment your choice.

You want to bring all the weapons you have at your disposal to fight what ails you. Then you can begin to work with your medicine to make yourself well, rather than just popping a pill and hoping that it does the work for you. (Please note that if you've been diagnosed with an illness, I don't want you throwing away the medication you've been prescribed . . . that's ridiculous because your body needs it! Talk to your body and mind *in conjunction with* taking your medication.)

Most doctors are trained to diagnose and treat sickness and disease either with drugs or surgery, but very few of them will tell you to fight it by talking to your body. They do know what part mental attitude plays in healing, for if patients scheduled for surgery have overly negative feelings about it or feel that they're going to die, physicians are apt to postpone the procedure until these patients get in a better frame of mind. Doctors just don't tend to take it any further than that.

It's not really the physicians' fault, since medical schools don't place any real emphasis on programming. If doctors *were* taught to simply work with the human body and its own defense systems and mechanisms, healings would be faster and more complete—and in certain cases, medication would be completely eliminated. It's funny, though, that a lot of doctors are remarking how people are becoming overmedicated. In addition, medicine that once worked years ago now isn't as effective because germs have mutated to withstand or negate their effectiveness. As disease becomes more sophisticated, we must start using additional weapons to fight it . . . and talking to the body can be one of the most effective.

Healing Yourself and Others

Be an active participant in your own wellness. If you see a medical professional, ask him or her about your affliction; learn everything you can about it; and then find out what you can do to make the healing process faster and more effective, such as additional exercise, a change in diet, or meditation.

When it comes to mental illness, know that almost all cases can either be traced to a breakdown in the bridge between the left and right brain or a reduced level of the substance known as *serotonin*. Address your mind and ask that your serotonin be elevated and balanced to meet itself and that the bridge from your left to right brain be absolutely solid. This tells your brain to heal itself by operating as it should, which will help stabilize mind function and performance patterns. Used in conjunction with any needed medication, this can be very effective in helping you return to normal functioning.

Everyone should talk to their bodies as often as necessary to maintain good health. Talk to your white blood cells to fight infection, talk to your T cells (which play an important part in your immune system) to up the protein count within them, and talk to your entire vascular system (which brings a fresh blood supply to all parts of the body in general). If you have a problem, talk to the area of the body that controls or affects that particular affliction. You might start noticing certain symptoms, so ask yourself, "What does the signal indicate is wrong with me right now? Am I hypertensive? Am I low on blood sugar?" Ask your spirit guides to give you information, even to the point of inquiring if you need to go to a doctor to be examined for a certain thing. Pay close attention to the answer you receive.

If you're attempting to heal others, have them help you with active participation—in other words, don't just let them sit there like a lump. While you're doing the healings, tell them to open themselves up to the healing energy and even send you their own energy, which helps in the process. Even if these folks are very ill, you can give them a transfusion of healing energy. *You will not get what they have.* When you receive their energy, you can thread it through your aura like a dialysis machine, cleanse it, and give it back. You can constantly urge them, "Work with me to heal yourself."

The mind and body are so powerful that they can create miracles. (I don't want to ever take our Creators out of the mix here because They must permeate into everything we do. And while Mother God creates miracles every day, other types of miracles happen all the time.) Let's say that you come to be a healer, which hopefully all of you will, for anyone can learn to heal in varying degrees. When other people approach you for healing, not only is it an exchange of energy, but they'll also come to you trusting that you have power. Since they've engaged that possibility in their mind, they're already receptive to your abilities. And you should believe in yourself just as strongly as they do.

❧ ❧ ❧

RESEARCH GROUP Q & A

Q: How long should a single healing take?

A: It can go very fast. You don't want to get into a long, drawn-out process because you'll wear the person out. This is supposed to be a healing experience, not a marathon run.

Q: You say that we should get people's permission before we try to heal them?

A: Yes, request that their will be engaged to give consent. Then ask, "Do you want to be well? Is there any reason that you can think of that you might have incurred this illness, perhaps as an excuse not to live in this life?" While this may sound harsh, it will make them think.

You aren't playing therapist, though; all you're doing is asking for these individuals to respond. If they can't think of a reason why they're sick, that's fine—it could be something they're not aware of, or it might be from a past life that they have no memory of. You just want your subjects involved as much as possible . . . you don't want to badger them, but you do want them to purge themselves of any negativity they're carrying. If they're in mental distress, you can ask, "Would you like to speak to me about this problem?" Sometimes just throwing it out there is enough to get them to vent and let the harbored bad feelings or hurt out.

Q: Do our cells speak to other folks' cells?

A: Oh, sure. That's responsible for what you call the "chemistry" between you, and it's also what causes you to become repulsed by others. Your cells are carrying on aside from you. Someone might remark, "Oh my goodness, that's the most attractive person in the world," and you go, "Ugh!" Your cell structure doesn't like the other cell structure, so it's saying, "No, they're not." People need to listen more to their body and mind. If you're repulsed by particular individuals, avoid them because there's usually a reason for it, whether it's a past-life response or a warning from your subconscious (which knows your chart) to stay away because they'll just end up hurting you.

Q: Is there a common thing that causes disease?

A: High stress! I've often said that certain types of stress are actually marvelous for the body, but you on Earth are being bombarded by the wrong type. Stress with a reason—that is, because of your job or something you're doing—is good. Impotent stress, on the other hand, is incredibly damaging.

Spirit guides know when you're in jeopardy: your emotions let out almost what I'd call a "banshee" wail. When we hear this high-pitched shriek from your emotions, we know that you're in danger. So when you get to the point that you're "screaming" with stress, you should really ask for your guide's help. Say, "With your help, you and I will calm this down. Close my aura and keep it near me for protection." Right away, your aura will quiet down. This is very much like scared children who begin to scream—they need someone to hold them and make them cozy and warm. Comfort yourself and calm your emotional stress, and realize that the mental strain you're under can adversely affect your health and well-being.

Q: What about new and unusual "health" products?

A: You may find all kinds of strange and foreign mixtures out there, and if they make you feel better, it's probably fine. I'd be very careful of things that aren't tried and tested, however. In the United States, the FDA is the only stopgap you have, and a lot of the herbs that people are taking haven't been tested to any great degree.

Sylvia was blasted many years ago when she said, "Many of these herbs contain arsenic"—yet it's recently been discovered that certain herbs do in fact contain traces of arsenic. Be careful and read up on what you're taking.

Q: Does taking estrogen harm women?

A: No, unless it's really high doses taken for an extended period of time. Estrogen is actually very good for women because it keeps them young longer, and it also protects them from strokes and heart attacks. Yet not every woman who gets to a certain age should think that she needs it just because all of her friends are taking it.

You need to monitor your own body. If everybody else is taking hormones, that doesn't mean *you* need to take them. If you're not having hot flashes or night sweats, don't take them. And if you *have* been taking hormones, lay off of them for a while and see how it goes. If you start feeling really crazy and very tired, then go back on them.

At this time there's a great deal of research going on regarding hormone replacement therapy (HRT). It's sometimes thought in Western medicine that HRT causes cancer and even makes women more prone to heart attacks. This is still not a proven fact, but many doctors are recommending herbal alternatives instead. It's certainly something you should consult your own physician about, and even get a second opinion if necessary.

Q: Do the rain forests contain herbs that can cure disease?

A: The world's rain forests contain plants that can cure almost any disease, but encroachment of civilization is putting them in serious danger. Since so many of these forests are being destroyed and cleared for profit, this can have serious ramifications as far as your planet's environment is concerned—but even more devastating is the destruction of flora that can be utilized for medicinal purposes. The so-called uncivilized tribes in New Guinea, Indonesia, Africa, and the Amazon have known about these plants and herbs for generations; their shamans and witch doctors use them in poultices and brews to cure tropical diseases and other afflictions that their people may encounter.

Not long ago, some people in Kenya got so sick that they became curled up into a ball due to muscle spasms and had difficulty breathing. They asked to see a witch doctor, who took one look at them and gave them potassium, which caused them to uncurl and breathe normally again. It turns out that the heat had caused these people to become so dehydrated that they suffered the effects of potassium deficiency. (If they'd had a Western doctor, he would have called it a seizure and ordered an MRI.)

Q: Is holistic medicine always the answer?

A: Well, God did make doctors, just as They made us. While I think that you have wonderful alternative medicines and treatments on Earth, I'm getting very frustrated that many of you are forgetting Western medicine altogether, which is absolutely ridiculous. People are trying to treat themselves with only herbal or unproven methods, and they aren't going to their doctors . . . and they're dying!

I've never been one for newfangled ideas at the cost of proven methods. Now, do I believe in magnetic healing? Yes, I do. Do I believe that crystals have some bearing? Yes—more than Sylvia does, by the way. Do I believe in mind over matter? Of course I do. But I also think you have to be very smart about going to a physician when something is beyond your power or scope. Use all of the alternative medicines and treatments you want, but do so with the aid of medical professionals. If nothing else, they can track whether these methods are working or not!

If your doctors are skeptical about some holistic treatment, point out to them that it can't hurt to go with something different if it works for you. Also, assure them that you'll consult with them on any dangerous remedies, supplements, or herbal concoctions; and that you want them to check your health often for progress. Your physicians will work with you, especially if you find that they're more open-minded, and you'll have the added benefit of their knowledge of your illness or disease. Then you'll have a nice mixture of Western medicine working in conjunction with holistic methods to effect a healing or cure.

Q: Why is it that those who are around sick people all the time don't tend to get ill themselves?

A: Because they're too busy helping other folks. They're constantly saying to themselves and their immune system, "I can't afford to get sick; these people need me." The tragedy is that society has always said to get plenty of rest, and the medical profession preaches it but doesn't always practice it. When you see those doctors or nurses on TV programs such as *ER* working incredibly long shifts, that's probably the most real thing about such shows.

Why should society make you feel that if you don't get enough sleep you'll fall over? If you get too much rest, I guarantee that you're going to be in worse shape because the body is not a resting vehicle. If it were, God wouldn't have made you with legs. When you think, *I must get 12 hours of sleep . . . I must take a nap . . . I must put my feet up . . . I need my rest,* your mind starts reacting to that programming. You have a mouth to speak, ears to hear, and eyes to see; you're an absolute activated unit. You may wonder, *But what if all I do is work really hard my whole life and then die?* So what? It's better than going to the Other Side after having lived your whole life as a slug.

Q: When I help people, I feel wonderful. What's the explanation for that?

A: The inner glow you feel is the same thing that happens if you're in love or carrying a child. Although we always feel this way on the Other Side, these are probably the only times in human beings' lives that they're devoid of self—the focus is totally either on the baby within or the lover without. Helping people also gives you this type of feeling.

Q: Does this feeling make disease bounce off of us?

A: Absolutely—anything that comes in the room would bounce off! That's the *chi,* or the life force that's so strong within you. But there's something else at work here: *endorphins.*

People who are always activated and moving toward a goal, whether it's to make other people well or win a tennis match, benefit from endorphins. In extensive exercise, have you ever noticed how you got to a point of pain, but then you pushed beyond it and felt as if you could go on forever? That's because your endorphins kicked in and created the "second wind" effect. On my side, we often see how endorphins coat the cells and anesthetize them so that pain lessens. We also see this coating effect with beta-blockers that help keep illness and disease from nerves.

Q: Do we set up resistance to this?

A: Yes, you've been taught that you can't move past pain. To work through these behavioral overlays, simply affirm: *I deserve to feel good, and I know I can call on my endorphins. Healing has now come about and is currently in progress.*

Q: Are some people more prone to depression?

A: Sure, and it's usually because they're on their last life. These individuals have been to Earth many times and are chemically, bodily, and cellularly prone to being depressed. It's just too many times on the battlefield or too many hairs of too many dogs that have bit them. I don't know of anyone on their last life who isn't besieged or plagued by some type of depression. I agree with Sylvia that it has to do with a terrible homesickness that they're always fighting.

Protein intake will alleviate depression, and it will stimulate the pancreatic area and serotonin levels in the brain. You'll find that it helps you lighten up.

Q: I'd like to know a bit more about acupuncture. What can you tell me about it?

A: Developed in China several thousand years ago, acupuncture is the use of tiny, thin needles to stimulate nerves and what the Chinese believe to be the "electrical" balance of the body. It has been found to be very effective in many cases but is considered to be an alternative medical treatment today and, as such, is not fully given credit by Western medicine.

Q: What are meridians?

A: In acupuncture, a *meridian* is a line of stimulation points in the body that directly relate to certain organs and bodily functions. The main meridian in the body contains the *chakra* points (highly psychic and cleansing points that directly relate to major glands and bodily functions) and runs from the top of the head to the groin area. There are hundreds of stimulation points in the body that are used by licensed acupuncturists to stimulate and heal afflictions and even cure addictions.

Q: Is there a meridian that grief travels?

A: Grief affects certain functions of the body, but it doesn't necessarily travel a given meridian because it affects people in different ways. Yet since grief can affect the major glands, the pituitary gland; the thyroid gland; and, in particular, the pancreatic area should be addressed. A lot of acupuncturists find that the sides of the palms help in treating glandular problems for some reason: they'll not only treat the stimulation point for the pituitary in the forehead, but they'll treat the upper sinus, then go right down into the throat chakra, and then finally treat the left and right outside palms of the hands.

Q: If we're grieving, should we tell our hypothalamus to release more endorphins?

A: Exactly! The endorphins will bring pain relief as well as mental stability. A flood of endorphins just makes you feel good.

Q: Is trouble in communicating with passed-over loved ones due to grief?

A: It can definitely be a hindrance. Let go of your pain and grief, since these are great blockers of communication. Get into the mind-set of knowing that your loved ones are very happy on my side, for it's impossible not to be. In that realization, let your grief dissipate . . . and you'll soon find that your loved ones start communicating with you.

❧ ❧ ❧   ❧ ❧ ❧

Chapter 8

Tips on Diet and Exercise

Francine: Now I'd like to talk some more about endorphins, which are the body's fighters of pain.

Scientists say that endorphins are chemical substances called *polypeptides,* which are created by the brain and sent through the neurological system to relieve pain. If you experience a physical trauma, endorphins will kick in and ease the agony of broken bones, wounds, and the like; but you can also program them to come to your aid and relieve migraines, back pain, muscular aches, and so forth. You can talk to them just as you would your natural defense systems, for in actuality they *are* a part of these systems.

Strangely enough, endorphins can also emit when you're in love. That feeling you get—you don't want to eat, you don't want to sleep, and you seem to be living on nothing but air—is very euphoric. And you can create something quite similar to that euphoria with exercise . . . provided you don't push yourself too hard.

How Much Exercise Is Too Much?

When you exercise, not only are endorphins released, but oxidation occurs within the body as well. This is a marvelous thing, since it helps you rinse out all of your toxins, just as you'd flush out old plumbing. Exercise should be done in moderation, however, as too much of it done on a regular basis can be harmful.

Scientists are now coming to a consensus that punishing workouts break down the body's immune system and collagen, and they weaken joint structures, too. So for those of you who want to run 20 or 30 or more miles every week, I'd be very cognizant of these facts or take the precaution of eating massive amounts of protein. I recommend against daily rigorous exercise because people can become hooked on the endorphin response of the body—that's why we hear about exercise fanatics.

Yet it's very important to get *some* physical activity because you're not of the pioneering stock anymore. Years ago when human beings used to tend their crops by hand, they'd bend and stoop and move constantly. You don't do that now, which is why you have to make a conscious effort to move your body. I'm not concerned with calorie reduction here; flushing out your body and optimizing your health are what matters.

Now, people will say that they get enough exercise during the day by pulling weeds or walking up and down stairs. No, that's not enough: you need about 15 minutes of solid aerobic activity to bring your heart rate up to the point that it does you some good. Since the heart is a big pump that flushes the blood, 15 minutes of exercise, three times a week, will give your system tip-top detoxification.

If you're looking to do some toning, I'd like to see you do so through an activity such as yoga or martial arts. If you want to do weight training, that's perfectly all right—unless you're trying to be a bodybuilder (which is a very small minority of people), you only need to use light weights and do rapid repetitions. And when you're working any muscle group, you must concentrate your mind on it or you won't get results.

To be in the gym for three, four, or five hours puts tremendous strain on the body and is certainly not healthy. If humans would watch what happens in the animal kingdom, they'd learn a lot about exercise. You see, animals use their adrenal area for fight or flight or for chasing after food. But you certainly don't see a lion or an elephant or even a dog or cat trotting down the street simply to work out.

To be sure, exercise does help you clear your mind. People who have anxiety attacks are very sedentary, so the best way to get rid of them is to *move*. The problem is, those suffering with these debilitating episodes get so immobilized that they don't want to go out and do anything; thus, they become trapped in a circle of pain, solitude, and fear.

You can work on programming yourself to get past this so that you can enjoy optimal wellness. When you exercise, tell your hypothalamus gland, "I'm going to take a brisk walk. When I do, I want the endorphins to kick in." Always address your body during exercise, particularly the parts of it that will respond: "As I walk, I notice that my arms are swinging, my hip joints are becoming very limber, my shoulders are in cadence with my step, and I am holding my head very erect. I am also flushing all toxicity and negativity out of my body, and I feel wonderful."

If you do so, you'll find that even if you only walk around the block, you'll get more benefit than someone who's sitting on a bike, grinding away for 30 minutes, sweating the whole time, and griping about the fact that it's so miserable to get into shape. When you just leisurely walk, swing your arms, and at least get your heart rate up to a certain level to rinse out the toxicity, you'll see better results.

If you're peddling a stationary bike and your heartbeat is only going to about 115 when others who are doing the same activity find that theirs is up to 150 or so, this means you happen to have a "relaxed heart" and low blood pressure, and there's not much you can do about it. Certain people are just this way, and no amount of exercise can change that (safely, anyway). Having low blood pressure and a relaxed heart are not bad things by any means.

The Food Equation

When you're exercising, you must eat at least as much as you were eating before you started. You might think, *I'll exercise and eat less*. That's a terrible thing to do because it won't decrease body fat. Rather, your body will think that you're in a starvation mode and immediately set up a warning to hang on to your fat or cellular toxicity. Keep in mind that you need a certain amount of healthy fat, particularly around your organs. It was meant to be this way: if you look at people in cold climates, they don't have a problem with putting on extra weight, but not to the point that it's unhealthy.

Women also tend to carry excessive poundage around their hip and thigh area, which is a very reasonable thing that God created because of the fact that females carry children. Although women constantly gripe about how they have a heavier lower part of the body, this was designed by God so they'd be sturdy. I don't care how muscular a man is, the tiniest woman usually has much stronger legs proportionately than any man does. The bones and tendons in a woman's legs knit together to form a solid base to support her in pregnancy and childbirth.

But do be careful that the pendulum doesn't swing too far in the opposite direction when it comes to weight. If you could look inside the body of individuals who are overly heavy, you'd note the large globules of fat surrounding their heart and organs, and it would make you sick! This yellow, goopy, clingy substance is quite disgusting. Once you saw a visual of that, you'd want to rinse it right out of your system. Think of a garbage disposal that you've got to clear of bad residue. Have you ever had a disposal that food just sat in? You walk into your kitchen and smell this stench! That's what's going on in your body . . . the fat is putrefying and isn't clearing out. You can program your body to "evict" those fat globules, however. As always, it will know what to do to bring you to optimal wellness.

⚬ ⚬ ⚬

Research Group Q & A

Q: Should we limit exercise because of poor air quality?

A: No. Going back to early Indian or African tribes—not to be facetious, but no one breathed more dirt than they did because they lived in teepees and mud huts, yet they didn't get lung cancer. Primitive tribes also smoked pure tobacco and never got cancer . . . it's the substances in the filters that cause problems. I'm not necessarily saying that smoking is good, but I *am* telling you where this pollution is coming from. I actually think that the most dangerous thing your lungs are exposed to are heating units, particularly since some of the older ones contain asbestos. Lead-based paint and the "angel hair" you used to put on Christmas trees can also be deadly.

The body adapts to its environment, and it will continue to do so as long as pollution doesn't get too out of hand. Besides, you're not going to find many places that have pure air anymore. The best locales are in your more remote and less industrialized regions such as Alaska, Canada, New Zealand, Siberia, Tibet, and most deserts. Many areas of the world do have fairly pure air, though—and the great thing about it is that as far as absorbing pesticides, chemicals, and waste goes, your immune system will acclimate according to what you've been subjected to in your lifetime. If that wasn't the case, humankind would be extinct by now. This goes to show how smart your cells are, and how they will survive at all costs.

The human body structure has grown to adapt over the years. When you look at the size of body armor in museums, you'll realize that hardly any men today could fit into it. If people in the Middle Ages were to see you, they'd think you were giants. Similarly, few of us could comfortably sleep in beds from 100 years ago.

Q: Does exercise help our adaptive abilities?

A: Absolutely. Believe it or not, nothing acclimates faster than the human being does. You have been poisoned and polluted with all kinds of exhaust and chemicals and have been putting *e coli* in your system for years (you don't know it, but you have). In your generation, you've probably overcome most genetic problems and diseases because of your medicine and the resistance that's been built up in your bodies. I'm not saying that you'll be immune to every single different mutant and viral infection that crops up—but even so, nothing can compare to the days when entire populations were almost wiped out by plagues and diseases such as smallpox.

I don't mean just a small percentage here: During the Middle Ages, much of Europe's population was decimated thanks to the "Black Death." During the influenza epidemic of 1918–1919 (known as the "Spanish flu"), 25 million people worldwide died. Past times have seen a great deal of the population die due to disease and plague: there have been cholera, malaria, and hepatitis epidemics; and today HIV and AIDS are taking their toll on Africa. The count goes on . . . yet you in the modern, developed world have every advantage and can increase your chances of a long, healthy life by eating right, exercising appropriately, and using programming.

Q: Is swimming as beneficial for us as aerobics?

A: Yes, swimming is very good because the water resistance is high enough for good exercise, yet low enough to decrease the chance of injury. You can actually go for a longer period of time because of this lower resistance. Water has always been known to heal and cleanse—humans seem to find a natural lightening ability in it, and it has a very relaxing effect on the mind.

Q: What can help stop calcification in the body?

A: A low-fat diet with plenty of protein: eat chicken, fish, turkey, and salads; and drink lots of water. Some fat intake is good for the body, but consuming a lot of fat in meats and cheeses will increase calcification. That's why I've always been against dairy products. I don't mind your taking calcium supplements because that won't contribute to calcification, but getting your calcium from animal foodstuffs will.

Using vegetable oil is good, but fish oil is even better. And don't worry that eating fish, eggs, or things like that will increase your cholesterol—in fact, I don't really buy into cholesterol at all. People are so concerned about eggs, yet they're one of your most perfect natural foods and absolutely fantastic for energy.

Q: Are ultrasound or electromagnetic devices helpful as well?

A: Yes. Magnetic force is better for using on the body, but you can employ ultrasound because it breaks down a lot of the calcification people experience, such as gallstones, kidney stones, bone spurs, gout, crusted shoulder, and bursitis. Of course, the older you get, the more you begin to just form pockets of calcification because it's part of the aging process. Like Sylvia has said, old age is like a tree petrifying . . . most of you will live longer than a lot of trees, so you can imagine the calcification that will go on.

Oil also breaks down calcium—using lecithin, primrose oil, garlic oil, or vitamin E can be particularly effective for loosening it—and should be taken orally. People are always rubbing things all over themselves, but products applied externally won't actually do anything. There are only a few plants that absorb directly into the epidermis, and I don't know why medical professionals haven't told people that the skin is a closed organ. If that weren't the case, everything that you brushed against or went near would be absorbed. Women spend a fortune on all those creams and things that really don't do anything worthwhile for them.

Q: Can too much vitamin E be toxic?

A: Unlike vitamins A and D, which also store in the liver, there isn't a toxic dosage of vitamin E. Nevertheless, some medical research has shown that excessively high amounts of vitamin E may cause certain individuals to have blood clots. With most vitamins, three times the recommended dosage tends to be safe, but you should do your homework before taking any supplement.

Q: I've given my fat cells an eviction notice, but they're not listening. Now what?

A: I'm not trying to be gross, but most cells don't want to come out in fecal matter—they just don't want to go. You have to understand that you're trying to uproot something that's been settled in there for a long time. They're going to fight you before they become homeless.

Speaking of waste, I've seen so many people overload on grains, bran, and nuts; and they're ruining their intestinal tract . . . it's not good. Those of you currently eating a lot of nuts, grains, and bran are making yourselves susceptible to diverticulitis because your intestinal tract is not meant for that much roughage; it just won't take it.

Q: But we shouldn't eliminate grains altogether?

A: No, you don't want to eliminate fiber completely because it helps with the body's flushing process. You want to balance your diet, but keep it high on the protein scale because your body is made up of protein. You never see a dog really thrilled about a chocolate-cream pie, and you won't find a cat going crazy about broccoli. (And the more you on Earth domesticate your animals, the more illnesses they have because they're eating like you. By eating what you eat, they become obese and get cancer—which are totally unheard of in the wild.)

Q: Is maintaining a balance the secret to good health in general?

A: Most definitely. A proper balance between diet, exercise, and positive thinking brings the best health. Some people exercise too much, and a breakdown of the body can occur; if *you're* a workout fanatic, be sure to follow a high-protein diet. Also, take amino acids and a multivitamin because you don't get enough of them in meat, poultry, or fish.

In addition, try to balance the bacteria in your body. All humans carry good and bad bacteria within them, but the body is such a marvelous mechanism that with positive programming, it can maintain balance—and optimal wellness—for your entire life.

Q: Francine, just how important is it to take care of our bodies?

A: It might be very strange to say that your body can actually get mad at you. But if you've abused it, it will in fact get angry and turn on you. It's like a group of people are housed within this community of your body, and you've treated them poorly. They're now rebelling and carrying picket signs in your liver. In other words, if you harm your body by becoming addicted to alcohol or some other substance, the cells will initially do their job of fighting but will very quickly cave in and start demanding more of the damaging element because they think they need more. You then feel like a slave to what your body wants—you've been taken over by the addiction, and you're no longer in control.

Your body is a powerful mechanism, yet it's also producing destructive "invader" cells all the time. You have every kind of cell in your anatomy that you can think of: hepatitis cells, cancer cells, tuberculosis cells, and other toxic or disease-ridden cells that could come alive at any moment. If you abuse your body, the cellular structure gets too tired of fighting . . . too tired of the stress . . . too tired of your submerging all this dark toxicity . . . and it just gives up. You allow these invaders to run rampant and terrorize your physical self, and the other cells that have been so depleted thanks to your mistreatment simply surrender.

But the body will respond magnificently if it knows that you're trying to take care of it. It will immediately say, "Oh, you really do love me, so I will perform for you." That's why only certain folks get cancer or other diseases, even though you all have those cells in your bodies. When you take care of your cells, they'll take care of you by continually fighting the invaders and not letting them reach your shore.

☙ ☙ ☙   ☙ ☙ ☙

Chapter 9

Conditioning for
the Mind

Francine: Even though we've talked many times about the mind and being disciplined in thought, I still find that some of you are having a hard time following a spiritual path. It's a very difficult process to condition your mind to get rid of obsessive, negative, and ill thoughts; but you need to understand that nothing can wear down your immune system faster than they can.

You may say, "But all the news I read or watch is so negative—how can I stop my thoughts from being influenced by it?" Well, if you look at things a bit differently, you can take that news and make it positive. Rather than concentrating on the bad in any given situation, start thinking about what good might come out of it. Try to remember the attitude of a woman who lost an arm. Whenever someone asked her, "Isn't it a shame that you lost your arm?" she'd reply, "No . . . it's wonderful that I still have another one."

Even natural disasters—be they earthquakes, hurricanes, or wildfires—bring some good along with the bad. People form new friendships, work together as a team, find strength in each other to go on and rebuild, and even learn to count their blessings more than they ever did before. Since life isn't meant to be lived in a totally protected state, negative things are going to happen, but sometimes they actually serve to make people stronger.

If you begin to think more optimistically, you will truly see amazing results in your life. Yet you can also affect the world in a positive manner by using prayer and petitions to Mother God and, most of all, by helping and setting an example for others. The more upbeat you become in your thinking, the more your health will remain sound and you'll protect the world from negativity. Think in terms of the world being a body just like your own: if you can program your body for better health, then you can help program the world to become more positive in nature, too.

You Shall Overcome

Just as our Creators rule over all of creation, you are a "god" of your own body—you rule all its functions and cells, and each cell resonates to your "godliness." All the cells in your body are subjected to your all-powerful mind, *but you have to use your mind* to control them and maintain good health. If you don't take care of your cells with clear and concise orders and attention, they can become mavericks.

If you've got the will, you can overcome any illness or disease. I don't care what diagnosis you've been given, if you've been told that you have the worst case of whatever, you can overcome it. First of all, *act as if you are well.* People will protest, "But it hurts!" Of course it hurts—life hurts! What's the worst you can do to yourself, strain a muscle or pull a tendon? What difference does it make if you're already in pain? Are you going to do more damage? No!

The next thing to do is to speak to your body in very literal terms. "I put this cold on notice—you have two days to evacuate" or "White blood cells, fight this infection or get rid of this disease" are a couple of examples of how to do this.

You can also ask for your temperature to be raised to burn out infection. It used to be that everyone wanted to lower temperatures, but modern medicine has recently come to the realization that having a high temperature isn't necessarily a bad thing. While you don't want to spike to 106 degrees or above, 102 or 103 isn't a dangerous level. You won't feel good, but you've got to realize that

God made it so the body's internal furnace can burn out the bad stuff. It makes no sense to keep lowering that furnace and then utilize an alien substance such as antibiotics. I'm not against them, but germs are so sophisticated these days that you get an illness and they lick their chops. This is what freaks out scientists . . . to know that a germ could think and mutate to resist medication.

Be very diligent in disciplining your mind against negative programming, for it will help your immune system. Notice how many times during the day you say "I'm tired" or "That's exhausting." What's really exhausting is that you're dealing with all of these negative thoughts, which won't necessarily kill you, but they do wear on the soul. When your soul becomes depressed, an entire chronological sequence of events happens: your entire body takes a hit and you're more apt to catch a cold, have disruptions in your intestinal tract, and get headaches; and then all your glands become disrupted and begin to function improperly.

Depression stems from dealing with "What if?" issues: *What if I can't work? What if I don't stay married? What if my kids hate me? What if I can't pay my bills? What if I go into a coma? What if I die?* Every time you get a "What if?" in your mind, it's best to order it to stop. You can also go a bit further by asking yourself, "So, what if?"

Of course if you listen to the messages you're continually receiving from your diabolically negative society, you'll become convinced that the world is going to hell in a handbasket. You'll become certain that you're going to suffer some horrible death at the hands of a viral infection, be brutally murdered in your bed, or face some other awful demise. Or, if you do manage to survive, you'll live out your days in a tragic, impoverished way, pushing a cart down the street while everybody throws spitballs at you or whatever you might imagine.

However, most of what you've fretted about in your life has never come to pass. As Sylvia says, "If everything happened that you anticipated, you wouldn't be sitting here now. You would have died a long time ago." The bottom line is that all of you ultimately *are* going to die, and then what you're so worried about won't mean anything anyway. If the worst-case scenario is that you pass over to the Other Side and have a great time, what in the world is so terrible about that?

You get caught up in the little negativities of life and let them affect you too much—why do you allow yourself to suffer so? Let's say that one of your "What if?" concerns comes to fruition and you're told that you have a terminal illness. You have two choices here: you can either negate this label and be happy for the time you have on Earth, or you can sink into a black hole of depression and despair. Do I mean that you shouldn't have medical treatment? Of course not. But do keep in mind what Sylvia always says to the folks she sees who are terminally ill: "Please look at this as an inconvenience. It's something that has disrupted your life for the time being. It's a doorbell that's rung while you're in the middle of a wonderful conversation or a movie. You're aggravated by it . . . no more, no less. It's a mosquito bite on the arm of God. That's all it is."

What she means by this is that everything is transitory in this life and will pass in its own time. If you're more positive, your health will improve in proportion to how you genuinely think and act.

Dealing with Pain

You can use your mind to stop any pain you're dealing with. Think about people who have lost feeling in areas of their body that were affected by a stroke. If the body's biochemistry can do that, why can't you? I don't mean having a stroke, of course—but why can't you learn to mentally "cut off" that part of yourself that's in agony?

Please don't ever ignore your pain to the point that you refrain from getting help; after all, pain is a transmitter of information, an indicator that something is wrong. I don't want you walking around with a broken neck saying, "I'm defying this." You have to be very diligent about pain because its sole purpose is to warn you.

Any serious injury usually requires medical attention, and it should be sought. Seeing a physician is also appropriate for any discomfort that either hasn't been diagnosed or can't be explained. Most of you don't go to the doctor for minor burns, cuts, or scrapes—you usually take care of them yourselves with a Band-Aid and an over-the-counter salve or ointment to prevent infection, and that's fine (unless infection becomes a problem). However, I urge you to use your common sense because even the smallest of wounds or injuries can become very serious if not cared for properly.

Once your pain has been thoroughly diagnosed by a doctor and you've found the reason for it, you can begin to utilize your mind for relief and healing. Since your mind is the ruler of your body, in order to heal quickly and stop hurting, it needs to be a *good* ruler. If you don't use your mind to control the cells in your body, they'll govern themselves and depose you! So the first thing you'll want to do is make sure that you take charge of your own body with your mind. Be forceful; don't be afraid to give your body orders in no uncertain terms.

When you talk to your body for healing or pain relief, make sure that your words are as simplistic and strong as possible. So if you get a burn on your finger and it develops a blister, tell it, "You're not going to get infected . . . that's the end. I know I'm doing all the right things, so go away now! I don't need this, and I don't want it!" If you're in command, it will heal very fast, without infection of any kind.

Or suppose you've severely sprained your left ankle. Your doctor has wrapped the ankle and told you to put it on ice, but it's still throbbing in agony. Affirm: *All the cells in my left ankle work together to heal it as quickly as possible by repairing any sprained ligaments, muscles, and tendons. All cells reduce and eliminate the pain as much as possible, and all nerves in my left ankle keep from sending messages of distress to my brain because I already know the cause of the injury and do not need to be warned!*

You might also avail yourself of other tools of communication with your body, such as meditation or self-hypnosis, for they are very powerful and especially effective for longer-term illnesses or diseases such as cancer or multiple sclerosis (as well as many others).

❧ ❧ ❧

When it comes to pain, one thing you want to watch out for is if it ever becomes *chronic,* a word that means something is ongoing. Sometimes, it can also mean to your doctor, "I don't know the reason for my distress." Once your illness has been diagnosed by a physician, realize that knowledge is power. You now know how to program your cells and defense systems to attack what ails you, be it chronic or otherwise.

If you do happen to have a chronic condition, however, you can turn it off. For example, if you get migraines every 17 days, the next time you get one, turn it off . . . it doesn't exist!

You may say, "Oh, that's beyond belief." No! We know that cures can be effected by hypnosis, so why couldn't you hypnotize yourself out of feeling bad? I'll tell you why. You're *conditioned* to have that migraine every 17 days, you're *conditioned* to have PMS every 28 days, or you're *conditioned* to have a cold every spring. You hear people say, "I get sick every Christmas" or "This is my bad time of the year; my allergies are going to flare up now." That's programming!

Your body will respond to how you think, act, and verbalize; so what makes you think that it won't follow your directives if they're negative? All of you need to maintain mind discipline by nullifying the negative and accentuating the positive in life. You'll certainly be healthier and happier for it.

❧ ❧ ❧

Research Group Q & A

Q: Are people conditioned to have good and bad days in astrology charts?

A: Yes. You're given "up" days, along with "down" days—that is, when your energy is at its worst or when you're more susceptible to negativity. I was always against biorhythm charts for this very reason: because they program people. I went right in the face of someone years ago in a research trance who was looking at Wednesday and saw that, according to her biorhythm chart, it was going to be a "down" day. This woman was programming herself to be down on Wednesday, and that's not a fair thing to do to anyone. People will say, "Winter is my worst time," and sure enough, they come down with the flu and are exhausted during those months because they've programmed themselves for it.

If you could just have access to an internal view of your body, you'd see exactly how this marvelous mechanism works in its entirety, most of the time independently of your mind. What you really need to have is your body working *with* your mind. Your mind is the ruler, and the cells are its subjects, and you certainly don't want them running amok. You've probably taxed your subjects too hard—not through work, but thanks to the lack of mental discipline in keeping your body healthy. There's nothing more dispiriting than having a ruler who's always depressed, uninvolved, tyrannical, or negative . . . those are grounds for revolution.

Q: So how much influence does programming really have on our health?

A: Programming, and the acceptance of it, can make all the difference in whether we're healthy or ill. You not only have to deal with the continual messages you receive from society, but with your internal programming as well . . . and you can be your own worst enemy. For example, if you say, "Of course they can do it, they're younger than I am," or "They can heal faster than I can because they're children," this is all the wrong type of programming.

One of the most effective techniques for positive programming is hypnosis because it can take you back in time. You don't necessarily have to go back to a prior incarnation, although you may eventually want to do so. Rather, go back to the time in this life in which you felt the most energetic and healthy. When were you at your peak: was it five, ten, or twenty years ago? Now have the hypnotist say, "With that cell memory, we're going to re-create that healthy period in your body right now in this time. Bring it straight up and utilize that cell memory to make any adjustments that are necessary for optimal wellness."

This not only brings up cell memory of perfect health, but it also tells your cells to bring that memory to the foreground and duplicate it to effect a healing.

Q: How can we use our minds to overcome physical problems?

A: Sylvia had some loose teeth once, and her dentist told her that they needed grafting. She said, "No, they don't. I'll fix it!" She made a conscious decision to simply say, "No, they are not loose, and they will not be loose. They will be fine." When she went back in for a checkup a month later, they were as solid as the rest of her teeth. The dentist said, "I can't believe that they aren't loose anymore!" To this day, he still talks about that.

Another time, one of Sylvia's teeth busted off in her hand. She went to her dentist quickly because she had to go on television, and she asked him to just glue it in. He said, "This will only last you a week or two." She simply stated, "No, it will last forever." He reiterated, "It's a temporary fix, Sylvia. When you drink anything that's hot or cold, or if you eat a steak or something chewy, it's going to come out again." Years later, that tooth is still "glued." When she went back in to see the dentist for a cleaning, he said, "Oh, you had someone else take care of it." When she insisted she hadn't, he couldn't believe it and asked, "What did you do to it?" She calmly replied, "I 'cemented' it in myself." This is not a miracle; this is mind over matter!

Q: Then Sylvia's will and desire combined with emotion to make her tooth well?

A: If she believes that the molecular restructure of that tooth has taken place, then it has indeed taken place for her. And never once has she thought about the tooth again—it's done and over with. If she went around saying to everybody, "I want you to look at this," and was always favoring the tooth or thinking about it, I guarantee you it would have broken off long ago.

Q: Francine, would you please explain the difference between will and judgment?

A: I *will* something to happen, and I *judge* the fact that it happens. Judgment is a very strong declaration—the gavel drops, and it's done; but the will can be wishy-washy—"I wish I did . . . I will try."

The word has been grossly misused, but your *will* is something you exert to create action or emotion: "I will do it" implies that action will be taken. Judgment, on the other hand, is very static because it's made: "You are now judged," "You'll be going to jail," or "You'll be saved." It's less active than it is abstract. So you can say that will is more emotional, while judgment is more intellectual. Judgment can also be emotional, however, when it comes to things such as bigotry.

Q: What comes first in healing, will or judgment?

A: The will should come first because you want to get the culprit that causes the illness, which is emotion. You want to use emotion *for* you, not against you. Saying things such as "I will get better" or "I will surmount these odds" are positive affirmations that speak to the body.

Be forceful and emphatic, and even use anger to augment your feelings and willpower to fight any illness.

Judgment comes later: "My judgment is intact. I know that I am already past this and am already healed." What you always want to do in any illness is take yourself to a time that's ahead. For example, saying, "I'll give myself exactly one week [or even one day] to get over this" uses both your will and judgment.

Q: How does this tie into addiction?

A: You can put your cells into action to rinse out any addictive substance with your programming and willpower. What makes addiction so bad is that the substance stays within the cells . . . and then, of course, they want more.

Whether you realize it or not, the greatest addiction you have on Earth is sugar. You may ask, "What about alcohol?" Well, alcohol is sugar—and nothing races through your world more strongly than it does. Cocaine and methamphetamine also make everything in the body race, thus giving you a false euphoric high and setting up a very powerful addiction.

The desire for any high comes from your cells' insistence that the effect makes them feel good, and they pass on their feeling to your brain. Yet you can use your will and desire to beat that feeling, strengthening them by recognizing the many problems associated with addiction: expense, unemployment, and crime; not to mention the hurt and anger you impose on loved ones.

If you really want to break down the worst addictions like crack and cocaine, tell your cells to rinse the addictive substance out of your system, and then enlist your will-power to keep you from taking it into your body again.

When it comes to addiction or even illness, change your point of view by taking the attitude that you don't want to be bothered with them and that they're ultimately inconvenient.

Q: Can role-playing help with healing?

A: Role-playing is a great way to release negativity. For example, you can have a good friend play the part of a mother while you portray a child. She'd act out however she wanted to as a mother, and you'd respond any way you wanted to as a child. The amazing thing about this is that your friend might start out being her own mother, but all of a sudden she'll jump back to being the mother she wants to be. Meanwhile, you'll take on what you know in being childlike, possibly even playacting how you'd feel as your own kid, which gives you greater insight into how he or she really feels.

Switching roles can be great therapy for parents and their children, helping them work out any issues they're having in communication or behavior. It can also give parents insight into how their children (especially teenagers) react, as well as how they want to be approached to share and communicate feelings and problems. When they play the role of a parent, kids also come to understand what their mother and father have to deal with.

Q: Don't psychologists tend to use this type of therapy?

A: Yes, but they don't go far enough. Mental-health professionals tend to think that every problem comes from this life and spend a lot of time talking about these silly "passive" or "repressed" memories. How do they know that past lives aren't responsible for such memories?

To give you an interesting example, years ago Sylvia closely followed a case involving a young woman who claimed that her father had killed a friend of hers. As Sylvia was watching the case unfold, she kept telling me that the father didn't do it. So, for her peace of mind, I did some investigating and found out that this young woman's repressed memory actually came from a life she lived centuries ago in Tuscany. In that life, her friend was her sister, and she'd become pregnant. This was a horrible scandal for this very well-to-do and elitist family in Tuscany, so the father picked up a rock and hit his pregnant daughter in the head and killed her. While this was a horrible thing to do, don't you see how funny karma is? Here we have the same father and daughter; the friend, who was also a daughter in the past life, is murdered both times; and the daughter's repressed memory from hundreds of years ago convinces her that her father did something in the present when he really did not.

What happened here was that the karmic door swung wide open due to repressed memory, and the daughter saw her father kill the same soul in a past life, and then she transferred it to the present. It may seem unfair to you that the father has to suffer now, and you may even wonder, *What's wrong with that awful daughter?* We can't really judge either of them, since they were working through something that happened long ago.

Q: Do psychologists help with memories at all?

A: Unfortunately, many of them are making a lot of money on so-called repressed memories. If you could eavesdrop on some of these sessions, you'd hear that the patients aren't actually relating these memories—they're being guided into them by their doctors.

I'm sure that any one of you could go under hypnosis right now and find out that in some part of your mind you feel that you've been abused, but it's not even from this life. It would be terribly, terribly wrong to go and point a finger at a parental figure because of a past-life memory of being abused. You're getting into very dangerous quicksand with that.

Q: So it doesn't matter whether a memory is from now or then—we should just release it?

A: That's absolutely true. It's too bad that lawyers get their hands on these repressed-memory cases and so many people become falsely accused. Mental-health professionals should be more spiritually attuned to the possibility that memories don't just spring up from this one existence. That is, instead of saying, "Oh, we have a case of abuse here; let's call the law in!" they should investigate whether the abuse was from this life or another. If it's from a past incarnation, then psychologists have no business getting other people involved.

You can become quite paranoid when you realize that any of your children may grow up and suddenly claim that you've abused them, and you might get thrown in some kind of confinement just based on somebody's word. That's a dangerous "Big Brother" way to live.

In the case involving the father and daughter that so fascinated Sylvia, "experts" who were out to make names for themselves started to get together and spout all this stuff about repressed memory. The law was called in, and the father went through a tremendously difficult time. While the court ultimately exonerated him, he suffered defamation because the case was high profile. And even his own wife believed that he'd killed their daughter's friend—until common sense prevailed. She's now fully in her husband's corner and knows he didn't do it.

As the case unfolded, it was indeed discovered that the memory the daughter had was from a past life. When this young woman happened to fling her hand above her head, she said that the whole thing came back to her at once. This simple act brought back the memory of her father using a rock on the head of her sister in a past life.

That's very much what you all do . . . like *déjà vu* in the truest sense of the term. You'll move a certain way or see something in particular, and anxiety and panic hit seemingly from out of nowhere. It's because you've touched the heart of a cell memory or a morphic resonance. What you must do when this happens is stop—don't run from it—and say, "What precipitated the action right before this? What was I going through? How did I feel about myself?"

I don't want to make you so conscious of your body that you become a hypochondriac, but being aware of your body and its needs are vital for healing and deprogramming. There's often a higher purpose to illness, so if you keep having recurrences of the same one, what's your body trying to tell you?

You have to ask the questions to get the answers: What was the thing said to you one or two hours before you started to notice that you got a sore throat or bladder infection? What was happening to you two or three months before you got the diagnosis of cancer, heart trouble, or high blood pressure? What were you doing prior to when your knee or your arm got hurt or when you caught the flu? What were your thoughts right before you became ill or injured? Take this further to find what's defeated you in the pursuit of success or a particular goal: What words came to you that made you give up? What words can you now say to make yourself negate this defeat?

When you become a master detective, you open up all kinds of vistas to yourself and become so magnificently aware of your body. Be like Sherlock Holmes, but investigate *yourself.* You're like a mysterious and fascinating house, and you should learn everything you can about that place you call home. If you knew termites were in that house, wouldn't you try to fumigate it? Well, you've got metaphorical termites running all over, and you need some "spiritual fumigation."

So who cares if the memory that's causing you so much pain is from this life or life 24—release it, and move forward with optimal mental wellness!

Q: Is it hard to get your mind to control your body?

A: Learning to condition and discipline your mind can be a long process, but it's actually natural for your mind to be in control. A few things do help with this, though, namely *willpower, belief,* and *positive programming.*

For most of you, just getting sick will give you the willpower to overcome it (unless you want to remain ill for attention, martyrdom, or the like). Positive programming is also fairly easy to do, for once you realize the negativity around you, most of you will just refuse to acknowledge it. The belief factor is probably the hardest for you because you've been programmed not to have it. You may want to utilize certain thoughts to augment your belief, such as, *I must survive for my children or spouse* or *I <u>have</u> to accomplish this—incapacity is not an option.* You could also turn to support groups to help you with your belief and willpower. All of these are outstanding tools and should be used if necessary.

One of the best tools of all for mind conditioning is self-hypnosis. This technique is easy to learn and doesn't take that long to do, but it can be extremely effective because you're speaking directly to your subconscious. I recommend that all of you make a recording of your own affirmations and positive programming to address your cell structure because nobody can do it exactly like you can. You can also use self-hypnosis to increase your brain power to become more focused at work or to get a better job.

The mind is the ruler, and you're creating it to be more powerful. Is this ego? No, that's not what's driving you. Rather, you're rising to the point of being a mentor so that you can help other people. When you do, you create miracles because of the positive spiritual energy that you're sending out.

Q: Do we fight negative programming by getting into our "spirit self"?

A: Yes. Once you lose that "basic self" that's keeping you earthbound, the creative form of you (that is, the God inside of you) will be able to leave all negativity behind. So if you have a prostate problem or eyes that aren't as good as they should be, your spirit self will remind you of your limitlessness and help you overcome your affliction. Like I've always told Sylvia, "You have no idea of the power of every human being to create; you're all the offspring of the Divine."

I'm reminded of the woman who was told by her doctor that she had a very suspicious lump in her breast. With vehemence, she screamed, "*No!* You don't feel anything!" Sylvia kept track of her and found out that she in fact didn't have anything wrong with her breast. Be like this woman and confront the issue! Don't meekly say, "Oh no, I don't"—emphatically protest, "*No!* I don't have this heart problem! I don't have this cancer! I don't have this fibromyalgia! I don't have it, I don't want it, I don't accept it!"

You have to confront issues and negative programming to make them disappear. What's wrong with so many religions is that they've never let you get angry. Anger would mean that you're confronting something, which means that you wouldn't be very easy to control. Of course if you're controllable, you're then submissive; passive; mealymouthed; and, as Sylvia likes to say with one of her favorite words, a "wussie." When you take control from those who want to control you, then you have the power in your own life.

Affirm: *The creative force of my spirit self has no connection to my basic self except to let it just move on its own for survival.* That's all you need to do to get in touch with your higher self.

Q: Are words really that powerful?

A: To the mind, they most certainly are. Christ used the spoken word to enhance his power, through phrases such as "Your faith has healed you." He cured many who were sick or diseased so simply that everyone was amazed by his abilities. What he was saying was just "Get rid of the basic self; leave it behind. This is a mortal coil that's only a facsimile of reality." He said this constantly when referring to "the kingdom of God" and through his assertion that if we were like children, we would understand . . . but few of us are.

Just as I did until I learned better, you make this mortal coil such a reality. You fill it with so much pressure and so many tireless challenges, and you give it a lot of credence that it doesn't deserve. It's like trying to make a car human—you're making this stupid vessel so important.

Q: You say that pain is a sign. Can you explain this further?

A: If you're hurt, it's a signal that something is wrong. Some people are born without any neurotransmitters and they're very much in danger—they can put their hand on a stove and burn themselves practically to a crisp, yet they don't know it until they start to smell burning flesh.

Do take care of your pain by verbalizing to your neurotransmitters, using pressure points, or practicing meditation and visualization. But if you're in agony, don't try to diagnose yourself! You've got doctors for that, and they should be utilized.

Once it's been diagnosed, and the doctor has said, "There's nothing more we can do for you," you can take that pain and put it away from yourself. Think of your pain as a ball with spikes on it (or make it as ugly as you want). Put it in a box and then blow it up. I guarantee that if you do this enough, your pain will come right out of you.

It's important that you don't keep acknowledging your ailments. Every time you say, "Oh, I can't do that because my old problem is coming back" or "My knee has always been weak," you're implanting another negative cell memory. Instead of just complaining, become aware of what your body is trying to tell you. What kinds of activity don't you want to do anymore? Your higher self probably wants to do these activities, so why is your basic self holding you back? What kind of morphic resonance is giving you tendinitis, carpal tunnel syndrome, a ligament pull, or whatever?

When you come back to the basic self and cell memory, you can readjust. Let's say that you're tired of carrying excess weight. Break down that cell memory of hiding, of being a porpoise that's trying to swim through the thick goop of life. What is your basic self trying to protect you from? Perhaps it's a "carnivorous" person you're with, or some draining entity that you're trying to protect yourself from. Once the diagnosis of your life has been completed, you'll be able to overcome the limitations of your basic self and easily rise above negativity.

❦ ❦ ❦   ❦ ❦ ❦

Chapter 10

How Important Are Genetics?

Raheim: Genetic engineering is going to become more and more prominent in the curing of disease and illness—eventually it's going to solve the riddles of cancer, AIDS, MS, and Lou Gehrig's disease. Now, if genetic study stays in this realm, that's great, but if it goes further, it could lead to a type of Atlantean science that's too technical and not oriented toward humanity. You see, things got to the point in ancient Atlantis where they were creating literal monsters by mixing together the DNA of different living species.

Similarly, the Nazis played around with genetics, using the Jews as experimental fodder and doing terrible things to them. It's the most amazing thing: human beings can't stop at doing something good; their greed carries them all the way to the edge of bad. In fact, the devil isn't someone who rules a supposed hell . . . it's greed.

Geneticists are going to start having great success by introducing healthy, immune genes into infected bodies, and those healthy genes are going to reverse entire genetic patterns to effect cures. Thanks to this genetic cell manipulation, you'll ultimately have cures for cancer and AIDS. The only problem is that they're going to be solely available to the rich, which is very sad, but they'll be the only ones who will be able to afford such cures. There's also the very real possibility that geneticists will get crazy and start doing things like cloning, which could raise questions of morality. This can then lead to further experiments that border on those that were done by the Atlanteans and the Nazis. The science of genetics cannot be allowed to go in this direction.

In the upcoming years, there will be few things that can't be cured with genetic implants—from diabetes to MS, cancer, and fibromyalgia. However, these implants won't be able to stave off viral infections, which are most likely to bring down humankind. Unless people start taking care of the environment and stop cutting down forests, you'll see mutant variations of "old illnesses" such as tuberculosis and bubonic plague reappear, and they will wreak havoc. Geneticists will try valiantly to keep you protected from these viral diseases, but Mother Nature will still unleash her fury and make it very difficult.

Nevertheless, humans have always lived through these types of things, be they outbreaks of typhus, cholera, or diphtheria. Even in the Middle Ages, when so much of the population was wiped out because of the Black Death, there were still some who rose up with immunity, and humanity survived.

Whatever the medical community will not be able to do, you *will*. For example, your mind can rejuvenate your entire genetic makeup through cell memory. You can do anything with the human body.

How many times have you heard the old joke, "The operation was a success, but the patient died"? There may have been no reason for this individual to die, but that's where past-life recall, morphic resonance, and cell memory come in. They can give you a baboon heart and pig valves or perform every type of medical procedure on you, but if your mind says "That's it," your will breaks and you're gone.

Francine: Just like Raheim, I'm very, very interested in talking to you about some genetic research that we're beginning to see on our side. Although the science of altering cells by injection and other methods is in the infant stages, it will be of great benefit to humankind if it isn't abused. Very soon you're going to see some miraculous cures from genetic research . . . it's all quite exciting!

Cell memory and morphic resonance will also be utilized in the future, especially in psychology, but this field is not in a hurry to change its reliance on its demigods such as Freud and Jung. Psychology is also not predisposed to exploring reincarnation or prior existence; hence, progress will be slow except for the occasional maverick who uses the tools of psychic healing in his or her treatment and enacts cures. Sometimes it seems that "modern" medicine cannot see the forest for the trees.

It turns out that what you deem to be "primitive" on your side is often actually much more advanced than you realize. Native American culture, for example, is quite extensive and sophisticated. Members of the different tribes also routinely lived to be very elderly—on my side, we're convinced that's because they weren't subjected to a lot of negative programming.

Although the words *primitive culture* might seem to indicate that these people were stupid, they most certainly were not. The fact that Native Americans lived outdoors with nature and were very basic in their survival techniques probably made them smarter. And because their society wasn't complicated, it made them live longer—as a matter of fact, we've found that many so-called primitive cultures had longer life spans than the European cultures that were supposedly so "civilized." Isn't it amazing that the tribes that lived communally with nature, such as the Inuits, Mongolians, Tibetans, Africans, Pacific Islanders, and the like tended to live longer than Europeans and their early-American counterparts?

Today, the cultures of Western civilization are incredibly complex. Wherever you have a condensation of houses, work abilities, and people striving for what they want rather than what they need, you start getting much more into the stress factor . . . it's what you call in your slang, "Keeping up with the Joneses."

Why I'm going through this delineation of culture influences is important because, like genetics, it plays a role in your healing. Thus, when you address your body, it can help to say, "Whatever culture I came from that might have caused stress, I release all negative morphic resonance."

❦ ❦ ❦

When you're negating cell memory and morphic resonance, begin by nullifying the diseases or illnesses that you died of throughout your existence. To do so, go to one of your stress-free past lives and bring up the memory of the cell structure that was healthy and allowed you to live to a ripe old age. This will also help you in alleviating the strain on your cells now and insulate you from taking on a lot of negativity.

If you can gain knowledge about cell memory and morphic resonance in a hypnosis regression, utilizing that information can help you heal. Whether you're too thin or too heavy; or you have bad knees, a bad heart, a bad neck, or any number of other problems, there just may be clues to these conditions in your past incarnations.

Cell memory and morphic resonance can leak over like an inkblot in your personal life as well. If you had an existence in which you were impoverished, for instance, the fear of starving to death can lead to eating everything you can get your hands on in this incarnation. On the other hand, if you once had too much money and power, it can now lead to egotism and feelings of superiority—believing that others are beneath you—which affects body structure, mental ability, spirituality, and your social abilities.

Now, let's say that you were a nun, a spinster, a priest, or a very lonely sea captain in a past life. It may have affected you in this life, in that you're unable to interact with people; you're so tongue-tied and shy that you're trapped in a solitary existence. Or suppose you had an unrequited love affair in a past incarnation. I'm sure you know how damaging a love affair that didn't work out can be—well, take that experience into two or three lives, and the morphic resonance of it can result in feelings of paranoia, hatefulness, diminished self-esteem, and being too submissive. All of those things can come into play in your current life.

Not only can cell memory and morphic resonance make you feel suspicious and frightened of other people, but they can also be behind your pattern of continually picking the same types of "losers" who use you, take from you, and manipulate you. If you've been used to being celibate or unlucky in love in your past lives, guess what? The first person you meet in this life who shows you any sort of attention will make you feel like you're a kid in a candy store, and you may either put up with mistreatment or completely misread the feelings of someone who's just being nice to you but doesn't want a romance.

If someone doesn't want you, leave them alone. Please have the righteous dignity and self-respect not to chase after someone who keeps telling you no. After all, that can't be very bright spiritually. It's almost as if your ego can't stop asking, "Why wouldn't they want me? I'm so fabulous!" You may be, but you aren't for them. It's as if you keep pounding on a door that's locked to you, demanding that you be let in. You insist, "If you let me enter one more time, you're going to love me." Yet you put yourself in a rejection position by having the person whose door you're constantly pounding on tell you *no* over and over again. Go find another door!

Unfortunately, we women are typically the worst offenders when it comes to this type of behavior. It isn't our fault; ever since the Bible asserted that we're to serve men, we've been carrying that morphic resonance with us. We believe that we're supposed to be subservient; we're supposed to be seen and not heard, just like children; we're not supposed to have any ideas; we're not supposed to have any ambition; we're supposed to get old and inept; and, when we're young, we're supposed to produce babies and be quiet. This, of course, is wrong, but we carried these beliefs with us for centuries, until suffragettes started making headway for women's rights.

While we may even think that our genetics are behind such submissive behavior, women actually were revered in many early societies. This came to a halt with male-dominated religions, which quickly killed off the whole premise of a Mother God—and if you eliminate the concept of a Mother God, you have nothing to represent the female gender.

Yet even though society by and large is still dominated by men, women do tend to rule the household. And other than physical strength, females actually have more attributes to dominate than males do. For example, what woman hasn't used her feminine wiles to entice a man to do what she wants? It's important that we women always remember how powerful we truly are.

∾ ∾ ∾

Research Group Q & A

Q: Francine, do you believe in genetics?

A: Of course, but only insofar as human beings have preprogrammed what kind of genes they'd receive for their own specified perfection. But even with that, you can overcome your heredity . . . not to be disrespectful, but some of you haven't gotten a good shot when it comes to your gene pool. Others of you just didn't do too much investigating about it before you incarnated—you sort of popped in, looked around halfheartedly, and said, "I'll deal with all this later."

I want to add that it's so important you don't allow yourself to say things such as "Well, I knew I was going to get arthritic because my mother was" or "I knew I was going to become blind because my father did," since that's programming at its most negative.

Q: Does a baby absorb a mother's cell memory along with her genetics?

A: The baby does not absorb a mother's cell memory; she's just transmitting nutrition via the embryonic cord. And, of course, any baby gets its DNA from both his mother's and father's gene pool.

Q: Some twins act and think the same—is this genetics?

A: Partly. It's also due to the charts that the twins wrote because they wanted to come in as dual entities. When you're thinking about genetics, don't ever forget about your chart.

Q: When we plan a genetic defect in our charts, can we change it with our spirit self?

A: It depends on how you've written it in. Look at this in a broad scope: yes, everything is to be overcome in life, but the main thing you have to overcome is yourself. Whether it's fetal alcohol syndrome, genetic predisposition to heart trouble, bad knees, glandular disease, or what have you, you can absolutely readjust it. Your chart will govern the amount of readjustment you can make—you may be able to completely rid yourself of any genetic defect if your chart allows it, or you may only be able to improve your condition to a certain degree. In either case, improvement is improvement, so you should try to do it.

Q. I'm always hoarse, yet I don't smoke or have anything physically wrong with my throat. Is this just thanks to my genes?

A: In checking your past lives, I found that you were slowly strangled to death in one of them. In another, you were born without hearing, which caused muteness (you could read lips, though). You tried to form words and whisper them because you didn't know that you had a vocal cord and a voice. People couldn't understand you that much, but you certainly didn't know that there was any kind of vibration you could do with your throat to make sound. Those two situations together created the hoarseness for you now.

I know you feel embarrassed by people always asking, "What's wrong with your voice?" So rather than trying mints, lozenges, or sprays; let's release you from this condition. When you go to bed at night, vehemently state, "This phenomenon is ended *now!* I have released the slow strangulation and my muteness!"

Q. Are my recurring neck problems courtesy of a past life as well?

A: Yes, because you were guillotined. While this would have been bad enough, it was made even more traumatic because they decided to change executioners midway. The second executioner was in what they called the "Ale Shop" finishing up, and you had to sit in the hot sun with your neck in that hole and wait for the blade to fall for 30 minutes. The cruelty of that must have been excruciating—not the death, but just sitting there bound, kneeling in that position for so long with your neck on the block. No wonder it's given you trouble over the years.

If you're susceptible to tonsillitis, strep throat, gland infections, or any malady from the neck up, chances are that you've suffered trauma to the throat in the past. Say, "I release any throat trauma in the name of the Holy Spirit. Father God, take it away; Mother God, intercede; and Christ Consciousness, come and do a healing."

Many times physical conditions stem from both a past life *and* genetics. For example, Sylvia's voice has been hoarse because through so many of her lives, she was an orator, and orators tend to have what's called "preacher's throat." Yet it's also in her genetics to have a low and hoarse voice (and being a teacher and lecturer for so many years has certainly contributed to this).

Q. I have an enlarged heart. Where did that come from?

A: I usually don't go against the medical profession, but I will here. Some doctors claim that enlarged hearts are a significant cause of cardiac problems, and that's ridiculous. If you're over the age of 40 and you walk or move or breathe, you're going to have a larger heart than a 16-year-old does.

People who live at high altitudes also have enlarged hearts. However, you don't see elevated rates of cardiac disease in the Tibetans or Peruvians who live at high altitudes—in fact, their hearts are generally very strong and healthy. The only time you have to worry is if it's the size of a chicken's or is abnormally large. Be rational here. Since the heart is a muscle, the more you work it, the larger it's going to get.

Q. Is osteoporosis in my genes?

A: Doctors have probably told you that you're genetically predisposed to osteoporosis because it's the only way they can explain why someone becomes afflicted by it at age 40 while another doesn't get it until age 90 . . . and many don't get it at all. Osteoporosis is a condition that's usually associated with old age, but if you start developing it earlier, it could have nothing to do with your genes—it could very well be cell memory from a prior existence. It's important to tell your body, "If there was anything I might have died of that had to do with bones—be they broken, crushed, or whatever—I release it! It has nothing to do with this existence now!"

Q. So genetics don't matter at all?

A: Oh no, they do. Because you're in a physiological body made up of biochemistry, we can't leave out your heredity. It's vitally important that you address the fact that you've been genetically presupposed for certain dispositions, colorings, body structure, and state of health. Of course you chose to come into this body and take on its challenges, but that's not what we're addressing. You already know that you've chosen everything as far as your perfection scheme is concerned . . . but that certainly doesn't mean that you're prevented from manipulating your heredity.

I'm going to fly right in the face of science now. If your mother, your grandmother, or some other female relative had breast cancer, and doctors have told you that you have an increased risk because of it, you can change that. Your doctors are certainly giving you negative programming here, but they're not looking at it that way. Instead, they feel that they're warning you so that you'll take as many precautions as possible. They're right in a common-sense way, but do be sure to use that negative information to your advantage. Get regular checkups and mammograms and the like—but at the same time, go the opposite way and persuade your cell memory not to get into that kind of trauma.

Never believe a statement that begins, "You are doomed for . . ." Rather, use it as a challenge to overcome your genetic predisposition.

Q: Do genetic problems program us too much?

A: Absolutely. You can become so locked in to the programming that it does great damage to your soul. Statements like "My parents had this illness," "My grandparents died of that condition," or "I'm going to have that disease" get you nowhere. The more you talk about such things, the more they're sure to happen to you. That's programming.

It's so upsetting when I hear this type of thing from people on your side: "Everybody's teeth are supposed to fall out at a certain time." (No, they aren't.) "Everybody's supposed to have renal failure when they get old." (No, they aren't.) "Everybody's bones are supposed to degenerate." (No, they're not.) "I can't do this, I'm too old." (No, you aren't.) Stop blaming your genes or your age—in fact, stop surrounding yourself with so much negativity altogether—and use that positive programming to heal and stay as well as possible!

Positive programming can even be your so-called Fountain of Youth because by thinking young, you make yourself do things that you wouldn't ordinarily do. You push your "machine" to perform in areas in which you might have previously said, "After all, I'm getting up there in years, and I can't do this anymore." This is a desperate mind-set to get into, but you can overcome it, no matter how old you are.

Watch your language when you refer to yourself in a negative way: "I know I'm going to get arthritis because my family is arthritic," "I know I'll probably lose my eyesight because so many people in my family have," or any of those other "familial" concerns. The biochemistry can be changed in all of you, even if science hasn't shared that fact—if it weren't so, then no one would ever go into remission.

Think about this: a mother who has breast cancer has three daughters; two of them get the disease, but one doesn't. What's going on with the one daughter who stays well? Despite her predisposition for breast cancer, this woman had gotten everything "off her chest." That is, her two sisters took everything from their mother, packed it into themselves, and developed the cancer because they couldn't fight the negative programming and get it off their own chests. The disease-free daughter refused to accept what was written in her genes, so she was able to overcome it.

&&& &&&

Chapter 11

Alzheimer's, AIDS, and Other Specific Concerns

Francine: I hear Sylvia talking to client after client about negative programming. She keeps hearing declarations such as: "My father and brothers all died of heart problems when they were in their 50s. I'm getting into my 50s, so I'm expecting to drop dead soon." So guess what the words *expecting to drop dead* bring about? There's a complete change in chemistry that's created by fear, apprehension, and even denial. I'm not here to tell you that if you have a phobia, then you're automatically going to see it realized, especially if you verbalize your fear. A phobia that's kept inside is a dangerous thing.

During the great Black Death that swept across Europe and killed so many people, there were some who were immune to it—especially in the Jewish community. The theory is that because Jews wouldn't eat certain types of meat and were very clean, it resulted in increased immunity. I'm not saying that non-Jews are dirty; however, at that time in history, cleanliness wasn't prevalent in Europe (or in many other areas of the world), and surgeons were doing operations without washing their hands or instruments.

You may ask, "So were they spared because of cleanliness, or did they actually have some type of super immunity?" It was probably a little of both. Wrong or right, the Judaic people tended to believe in the Old Testament statement that "the good will be saved." So if folks really believe that they're good and blessed in the eyes of God,

131

they have more of a chance of a miracle happening to them or of being saved than those who feel that they're degenerate, despairing wretches. The Jews' spirituality and belief in God helped them combat the plague.

I do take issue with those religions and churches that promote the message that God in His wrath is heaping negativity, disease, and pestilence on humankind thanks to its unfit, unclean, or sinful members. For example, lots of folks still erroneously believe that AIDS has been brought forth upon the gay community because it's out of favor with God. What they don't realize is that this disease didn't start with gay people—it started with heterosexuals in Africa having intercourse with the green monkey, as well as by the explosion of drug usage utilizing "dirty" needles. No one heard of AIDS until just a few decades ago, which coincided with a tremendous upsurge of drug abuse in our society.

Homosexuality has been around since the beginning of humankind and was particularly prevalent in ancient Greek and Roman cultures, so why didn't AIDS start then? No, it arose thanks to modern society's use of drugs of all sorts and the corresponding sharing of needles that weren't sanitized. It seems that human beings can't accept the blame when negative things happen, so they're always looking for a scapegoat such as God or a minority group.

೪ ೪ ೪

Why are some people impervious to viral infections? Is it out of ignorance or because they're just immune to it? Well, a certain amount of immunity does come with genetics. But what's more important is someone's frame of mind and the ability to empower himself to overcome.

You can overcome anything you wish to if you elevate yourself to the point that you're not *in* your body, you're *above* it. The minute you allow yourself to become too earthbound is when you open yourself up to illness and disease, which is why spirituality is such a boon to the sick. And that's why miracles are always a positive affirmation of what's truly spiritual—miracles happen because you expect them to.

Speaking of miracles, you can certainly save other people from death, if they choose to be saved and their will remains intact. Yet I don't think it's always the most admirable thing to want to keep others alive, so it's not necessarily something you should be concentrating on.

For years and years, death was seen as the ultimate condemnation for a life full of sin. Since the Bible says that "the wages of sin is death," it was believed to be the worst thing that could happen to anyone. In actuality, the opposite is true. Therefore, a more appropriate saying would be, "The wages of life is the celebration of death." Death is when you get to go Home, so you should be looking forward to arriving at that destination . . . but there's also something to be said for enjoying the trip.

To make your trip of life better, start with your cell memory and anything from a past life that you've carried over—whatever is giving you phobias and terrors or is preying on you in any way— and release it. As for anything you're genetically presupposed to, just try to erase as much of that negative programming as you can. In other words, stop saying, "I'm just like my father: I have a temper just like him. I drink just like him. And I have liver problems just like him." Get that out of your head immediately!

If you find the fear flaring up that you're going to experience what your family has, immediately reaffirm by saying, "No, I'm not!" This is your hereditary challenge. To say that your mother suffered from Alzheimer's disease, which means that you will, too, is ridiculous—you have the power to learn from it, overcome it, and move on.

People in the insurance and medical fields will insist that if your parents died early, so will you. That is absolutely not true. Sylvia always likes to quote the case of Alfred, Lord Tennyson, who watched several of his siblings succumb to mental illness. Tennyson attributed the reason for his escaping this same fate to his friend

Arthur Hallam, whom he wrote about in his famous poem, "In Memoriam." Arthur was a cheerful, round-faced, wonderful person. (He still is, by the way; I saw him the other day.) Always positive, he'd say to Tennyson, "Come on, let's join the rowing team and quit thinking about whether or not you're crazy."

Arthur was like having a spirit guide in life, for he was Tennyson's caretaker and mentor. Strangely enough, his duty was to come down and be the catharsis for Tennyson so that he could write his wonderful poems. Unfortunately, Arthur died quite suddenly at a young age, but he saved his friend from becoming a victim of mental illness, and he made the poet realize that everyone has certain neuroses.

I can guarantee that if you put someone in a room and have enough people tell him he's crazy, he's going to believe it after a while, especially if he thought that those people had some authority. It's called programming, and you're all subjected to some form of it every day on Earth. Again, I must stress how critical it is that you reject these negative messages.

Mental illness is a subject that's very close to Sylvia's heart because she's studied it for so many years, not only scientifically but esoterically as well. She's convinced that entities who incarnate as bipolar do so to teach other people patience, kindness, and understanding. But I also know that these people may be getting certain types of psychic information that the world isn't comfortable with yet.

Sylvia always says that if she'd been brought into a family that didn't know what she was about, she probably would have been locked up. What she saw, knew, and felt as a child in the 1930s and '40s was not seen as acceptable then. It wasn't acceptable even in the 1970s—it's only been since the '80s that the view has changed. Of course prophets abound every day, and they always have.

❧ ❧ ❧

Research Group Q & A

Q: Does our vision and hearing worsen because of the aging process?

A: Yes. What causes vision loss is called "flattening of the eyeball," which is known to occur after the age of 40. When this happens, you either become nearsighted or farsighted depending on genetics. Start as early as possible to correct this by programming your eyes to be rounded out correctly.

Both vision and hearing start to deteriorate in the 40s; calcification starts occurring in the bony structure of the ear, and that's what causes hearing to go. Ask for it to be rinsed—as long as you always keep yourself in a state of rinsing and lubrication (by using lecithin, vitamin E, and fish oils), you can keep your hearing for a long time. One danger to hearing now is the volume level of music that young people listen to. Encourage your children to cut back on the volume, whether it's at home, in the car, or at a concert. Put earplugs in at any sort of musical event in which you have no control over the volume.

Q: My ophthalmologist said that most people get cataracts, but this improves eyesight so we don't need glasses. Is this true?

A: Oh, no! You must have misunderstood him—if you didn't, you'd better change doctors. Cataracts don't make your eyes better but create a foglike covering in your eyes that causes blurring.

Use the Bates method to help your eyes remain in tip-top shape. These exercises are very simple to do and use everyday objects such as a pencil or even your own hands. You'll probably help yourself greatly because people never exercise their eyes—they don't roll their eyes, they don't look near, they don't look far. Sylvia's grandmother Ada actually cured herself of cataracts when she was 84 thanks to the Bates method. (You can go to a bookstore or library to find a volume on how to do it.)

Q: What can be done for macular degeneration?

A: Talk to the "myelin sheath" to make the eyes healthier and to regenerate vision. The myelin sheath responds to neurological stimulus, just as fibromyalgia, lupus, and MS do.

Q: What about glaucoma?

A: Raheim advocates the use of rose water and glycerin, which have been used for eye maladies for centuries—Jesus himself employed them to help him heal the blind. Eyedrops sold in your stores won't really be of any help because they only last for a short period of time, but if you look at the ingredients in most of them, you'll find glycerin somewhere.

Q: Can cell memory help bladder infections?

A: As is the case with all illness and disease, cell memory is neither the cause nor the healer. In most cases, bladder infections are caused by bacteria. Don't be afraid to use a physician's help—it makes no sense to have a stiff upper lip and go through suffering just because you want to appear "strong." You have no idea what your nervous system takes from going through pain.

Of course you should employ positive programming here, but if possible, also take a series of sulfur drugs (sulfur is actually a natural substance, and the drug is its condensed form) to get rid of your infection. Then begin to build up your immune system so that you don't ever get a recurrence. The following can also help: Make sure that your iodine content is cut down. Drink lots of cranberry juice and water. Cut down on carbonation and caffeine. Stick with your herbal teas—the best ones are strawberry or peach, especially if they have psyllium in them (which most dietary teas do).

If you have to urinate frequently but don't have an infection, you may have a prolapsed bladder that you got genetically; start doing Kegel exercises (which were developed by Dr. A. H. Kegel to aid in childbirth, sexual enjoyment, and incontinence) to help with that issue. You should always see your physician when dealing with bladder problems.

Q: What can I do for the tendinitis in my arm?

A: Speak directly to your arm to get the blood flowing. When in doubt, remember that blood is really the lifeline of the body. Why do you suppose medical professionals take blood all the time? It's your body's barometer.

Q: What can we do about dyslexia?

A: Dyslexia is directly tied in to cell memory: it's not a disease; nothing is wrong with the serotonin levels in the brain; and there is no chemical imbalance. If you want to be specific, it actually comes from lives lived in Atlantis and Asia because people in those areas read from right to left, and dyslexia is a carryover of that.

Now before you say, "Here we go again into past lives," just remember that modern medicine doesn't really know what causes dyslexia. It's given to the psychiatric sector for treatment, which means that they cannot find any pathological or physiological cause for it. Psychiatrists can't find the cause either; they just know that it's a learning disorder in which numbers and letters are reversed and can't be seen by reading from left to right.

The most common treatment for dyslexia is repetition, and more repetition, and it usually works over a period of time. To teach people with this condition, keep going over and over the material to be learned, having them read and read again. A faster treatment would be a hypnotic regression in which they were deprogrammed of their past learning response (reading from right to left) and then brought back to the present time and learning response (reading from left to right). They'd be programmed to keep the same intellectual memory, but they'd be rid of the conditioned responses that were due to the past lives in which they read from right to left. These regressions are very effective and can even be done on children, with the optimal age being between 8 and 14 (depending upon the child).

Sylvia has considerable experience with dyslexia because she was a schoolteacher for so long, and she also discovered more than 25 years ago that there are rare cases of auditory dyslexia out there.

Q: How can we help children with ADHD?

A: ADHD (attention deficit/hyperactivity disorder) is similar to dyslexia in that it isn't a disease, modern medicine has found no physiological cause for it, and it's been relegated to the field of psychiatry. ADHD actually stems from someone being bored and lazy. Although the psychiatric community will say that it's due to behavioral problems not being addressed in a child by his parents, their treatments in this area are not always successful.

ADHD, which is far more prevalent in boys than in girls, can manifest in many ways—while it's a learning disorder, it can also become a behavioral disorder. Kids who have it run the gamut from being quiet and withdrawn to being hyperactive and disruptive. Some who have it are even misdiagnosed as being autistic because of their hyperactivity and acting out.

While some doctors use Ritalin to control children who have ADHD, this is a terrible drug. I wouldn't use

Ritalin on anyone! Similarly, Sylvia absolutely refused to give out prescribed dosages to any of her students.

You can help children with ADHD by realizing that they're not being challenged intellectually; they're also so accelerated in their own time and place that most people haven't caught up to them yet. They've manifested their frustration and aggravation by whirling around in a hyper manner and becoming disruptive. Hypnosis programming can be an effective treatment, as can the teaching of subject matter that stimulates them and keeps them from becoming bored, lazy, or unfocused.

In addition, you can try talking to their cell memory. Of course you can't just grab kids and take them some-place private to put them under hypnosis, but you can say, "At any time in your life, bring yourself forward to yourself and be where you were before, when you felt calm and joyful." Make sure you say "at any time" and don't concern yourself with whether they comprehend what you're saying or not—their cell memory will understand and respond, and that's what you're talking to. You can actually use whatever words you like, but do address their cell memory to go to a time when they were peaceful and happy and not so frustrated.

Q: Can we talk to *ourselves* to heal something like hypoglycemia?

A: Oh, absolutely. Ways to fight this also include small doses of high-protein foods during the day, staying away from a lot of carbohydrates and sugars, and eventually working your way out of it. Quiet your mind for better focus and concentration during your hypoglycemia, and if you become dizzy, just say to yourself, "I'm not going to deal with this now. I want my pancreas to start activating and give out the amount of insulin or glucose that I need."

Q: Can amino acids help us?

A: Yes, because they're a natural source of energy that goes directly into the system. Amino acids are found throughout nature, but there are approximately 20 of them that are necessary for the human body to grow and metabolize.

Your body produces some of the needed amino acids, but the food you normally eat can provide them, too. The essential amino acids that must be obtained from the diet are contained in protein foods such as meat, cheese, and eggs. Vegetables and grains provide only a portion of them, but not all, as the higher-protein foods mentioned do.

If you find your energy lagging, I'd take four or five tablets of a manufactured supplement that contains most, if not all, of the essential amino acids. There are several on the market, and I'm sure that you can find them in any health-food store. Many of these supplements can be found in the section for bodybuilders, as these individuals have known for years about the energy benefits of amino acids. Keep in mind that amino acids aren't stored in the body, so you will have to take a supplement daily.

Q: What causes spontaneous remission from disease?

A: This happens when someone engages his will so strongly that he rinses out the affliction. Lots of folks who are ill desire to be healed, but they can't engage their will strong enough to overcome the sickness . . . there's a very big difference between desire and willpower. Of those people who have gone into remission from cancer or other diseases, they usually used a combination of medical treatment, diet, and change of lifestyle—but willpower was number one on the list. And those individuals who know how to talk to their body make their willpower even more effective.

Q: When it comes to AIDS, is there a problem with the communication between cells?

A: The AIDS virus likes to go into T cells and create a hidden environment. Isn't that scary? It begins to set up house while camouflaging itself. Think of it as a colony of otherwise rational folks who have a Jim Jones or Charles Manson move in. He then invites his cohorts in and converts the cells.

Q: So how do we address those cells?

A: In your world, life imitates life. What you see outside your body is also happening inside your body: you see people out of control in the world, and you also have cells inside you that are out of control. That's what cancer is . . . out-of-control cells. Your own natural immune system fights them every day and usually kills them off, but such cells are renegades and won't go along with the program.

A virus is a serial killer that must be stopped by the cops, so to speak. The cells may think that the camouflaged murderer is only another anomaly and may accept it. It's so important that you get your army of white blood cells and red blood cells to fight that evil invader.

Q: Can the antibodies and immune system identify the disguised AIDS virus?

A: No, but you can take preventive measures for your body that are akin to brushing your teeth so that you don't get cavities. Every morning, greet the cellular structure of your physical self with this speech: "If there are any bad cells hiding, I want my body to kick them out! I'm still in control, so all healthy cells are attacking and destroying any bad cells, hidden or otherwise."

The only reason that someone would die of AIDS is because the disease's cells gradually invade over a period of time. Yet as long as that person has some cells that aren't invaded, they can be put into action and fight. That's why people have gone on for decades with full-blown AIDS—with the rest of the cell structure fighting the disease, they can last a long time!

Q: How can we deal with migraines?

A: We're getting into a very definitive area here. It appears that your entire vascular system is constricting, especially around the neck and the top area of your spine. You're cutting off the capillaries to your head, which is what gives you that sickening, "My head's going to blow off" feeling. Tell your body to increase the blood flow to the cranium and open the vascular system in the neck.

Q: When I have severe migraine pain, I sometimes lose touch with reality or fall asleep. What causes that?

A: The judgment and will centers in your brain have been totally shut down. What happens is that the pituitary gland says, "This person is in too much pain, so we're going to make her go into a near-comatose state." The pituitary gland is there to protect your body and will save you at all costs, even if it means shutting down some parts of your brain.

To come back to reality from migraines, have someone talk to you. Even if you're asleep, your pituitary and other glands are wide awake, so have the person tell your pituitary gland and vascular system to restore blood flow correctly and stop the shut-down process of the brain.

This shut-down process activated by the pituitary can also be utilized to bring back coma patients. In the past, people didn't talk to those in a comatose state—only recently has the connection been made that "If we talk to them, they can come back." So why do they come back? It's because everything in coma patients is listening, including the cells and glands. As long as it hears talking, the cell structure says, "Hmm, maybe we aren't dying" and will sometimes activate to the point where the individuals wake up.

Q: Why do severely disabled people sometimes forget to breathe?

A: They find it very laborious to lift their chests to breathe because they don't like being in the physical body. In many ways, that's why trance mediums down through the years have always had to have someone there to physically watch them. Margaret Leonard was once in trance in England in front of a group of people that included Arthur Conan Doyle, who was the only one who very astutely wondered aloud, "Why are Margaret Leonard's lips turning blue?" Realizing that the medium wasn't breathing, those she was sitting for punched her on the arm and told the spirit to breathe. It turns out that the spirit who'd been talking through her was going on like a magpie, so it inhaled deeply and profusely apologized.

We spirit controls have to be trained to do that. I remember when Sylvia was 19, for instance, and I had to make a concerted effort to breathe because I'd go for long periods and make these little gasps. Even to this day I have to remember to breathe whenever I come into Sylvia's body during trance.

Q: Why do we leave our bodies during illness?

A: You astrally project out and just go away because you don't want to deal with the malady. This also happens in hallucinations, along with instances of severe pain, fever, and migraines. In years long past, the old family doctor would help deal with sickness by sitting by the bed, bathing the head, and saying to the person, "You're going to be all right." You no longer have that bedside manner to help you deal with illness, and it's a shame.

Q: Are there specific areas of the body to address for healing Alzheimer's disease?

A: I'd focus on the neurons of the brain, since what happens in that disease is that the synaptic impulses are breaking down. Tell your brain, "Your synaptic impulses can now reroute themselves and keep firing."

When it comes to Alzheimer's and senile dementia, you should also address long-term memory to reactivate short-term memory. And you can speak directly to the cells and body about these conditions, for they break down in the brain cells. Tell your brain cells and synaptic nerves to regenerate and return to normal function.

Keep in mind that there is a very specific type of person who gets Alzheimer's—they're what we call "shut-down personalities." Now I don't want you to get mad and protest that your wonderful mother or brilliant father was not a shut-down personality. What I mean is that this is the type of person who holds things in, is very private in nature, finds it hard to interact with others, and is a poor listener because of the lack of feedback.

Q: Can we help those with Alzheimer's go back to a past time of positive cell memory?

A: Yes, but you want to catch them before the disintegration is total. There isn't any special time for which this is true, but do engage the will and the chart of the person. When you do this, it doesn't mean that you can forestall their ultimate demise or whatever they're here to do. You aren't interfering with that, but you're certainly going to make them a happier person until the end of their time here. You can relieve their suffering as much as possible.

Q: Will there ever be a cure for Alzheimer's?

A: Yes, but with most types of the disease, you're going to find out that the cure will have to be more etheric than simply one of vaccination. On my side, we know that it's viral, but no one has figured it out yet. It does have ties to genetics as well: chromosomes 19 and 21 are suspicious, but there are a lot of people with defects on 19 and 21 who will never get the disease. We've discovered that it's a viral type of infection that forms globlike burrs in the brain. And while some elderly may have senile dementia, this is different from Alzheimer's disease.

Q: Are organ transplants risky due to cell memory?

A: I don't believe that there's anything wrong with transplants. The only thing you must be aware of is that you're inheriting cell memory. But don't use the word *risky* because it's negative.

Q: Do some people reject transplants because their mind is saying, *That's not mine?*

A: Well, you see, all doctors do is try to get a match with your cells. They can get *close* to a perfect match and then become aggravated when the organ isn't accepted by the body. Rejection happens when something in the cell memory causes the pituitary, pineal, or thyroid to say, "We don't want that organ. It's got some bad memory to it that we don't want to be a part of us."

Q: Is there a better way than to be given all those drugs to suppress that rejection factor?

A: I'm sure that anyone in the medical field will tell you that such a reaction is only temporary. Yet if the body wants to reject an organ, you don't have much of a chance . . . I don't care how many antibiotics you use. Doctors who are within the "know" will say it's only a matter of time.

Q: How much cell memory can a transplanted organ carry?

A: Well, you must remember that a person's cell memory is contained throughout his body in every single part. However, organ transplants only use a small portion of that body and won't offer the full impact. For example, if you received a kidney from a concert pianist, you might find yourself with a sudden love of the music they played, but you wouldn't inherit the ability to play piano at that level.

Some people who have had a transplant find themselves liking (or disliking) previously unfamiliar things, such as getting cravings for certain foods that they'd never wanted to eat before. This isn't significant, though—it certainly doesn't get to the point where if you received a transplant from a serial killer, it would make you one or even make you think about killing. That's . . . what do you call it? "Hollywood stuff"!

❀ ❀ ❀   ❀ ❀ ❀

Chapter 12

Overcoming Morphic Resonance

Francine: You have a definite spiritual DNA that far surpasses anything having to do with your physiological DNA. Your spiritual DNA contains everything from your entire experience within it . . . and there's the rub. Many times you'll carry that morphic resonance with you—that is, the memory of all that's happened to you, whether it was done on a physical, emotional, or spiritual level. Living so many lives can cause you to absorb all of these very thick, cobwebby remnants of past horrors that Sylvia calls "behavioral overlays."

When you incarnate, your mind begins to set up a view that "what has happened before could happen again." On a lower level of consciousness, you try to re-create what's happened to you in the past, which is why many of you will experience different afflictions in your life. So if you only address your body, you're not going to get to the root of these afflictions—you must work with your soul. It's much like a glass of milk: once you drink it, the coating on the glass stays . . . the milk is no longer there, but the coating is. That's what is happening with your life's plan.

Let's say that in one of your incarnations, you died of tuberculosis at the age of 22. When you reach the age of 22 in *this* life, your morphic resonance reminds you that you're presupposed to this disease, so all of a sudden you begin to have asthmatic conditions and bronchial episodes. You may worry that your body is turning against you, but it isn't. However, since every one of your cells is a thinking entity unto itself, it has a mind of its own until the central station, which is the brain, takes control of them.

It's not the fault of the cells so much; it's very much the fault of familiarity. The cells remember if you've starved to death in a past life, for instance, so they keep you very heavy in this one in an attempt to protect you. And this "inkblot effect" spreads out to your relationships, too: if you were tortured in the past, it could explain why you feel as if you're being tortured in the present. It's important that you focus on clearing those old cobwebs out of your mind, and you can begin doing so by saying, "Whatever patterns I'm carrying over—be they in the area of health, wealth, relationships, career, or spirituality—must be stabilized and rinsed clean."

Your cells' morphic resonance sets up patterns for eons of time. (Such patterns don't remain when you go to the perfect environment of the Other Side, but they come back when you incarnate.) It would be akin to your getting sick every time you eat at a particular restaurant or feeling uneasy anytime you walk into a certain room. When you notice that you have the same strong physical reaction to a particular situation, ask yourself why: "Why do I feel uncomfortable driving in traffic?" "Why do I hyperventilate when I'm in a high place?" or "Why do I have so many irrational fears concerning my children's safety?"

Now, although you may get some intuitive insight while conscious, you're more likely to find the root of your problem in a meditative or hypnotic state. Your subconscious mind knows the reason for your distress, and you only have to contact it to get the answer. For example, if you become anxious when you're in a crowd and don't know why, ask yourself, "Was I caught in a mob in a past life? Was I trapped in an enclosed place with many people, such as in a cave or jail? Was I manhandled, injured, or killed in a riot or stampede?" You may even get a vision that explains where your fear or phobia comes from; if any anxiety surfaces with it, simply state, "I only want to observe this; I do not want to relive it."

Lots of you have also been afflicted by illnesses that are no longer around, and that's why so many ailments are undiagnosed now. There were all kinds of ancient plagues, along with scurvy and rickets and the like, which are no longer part of your society. The doctors of today aren't aware of what you might be carrying in your cell memory. For example, some of the people who have fibromyalgia suffered from terrible rickets (a condition that alters the body's growth structure as well as its soft tissue) in a past life. Likewise, those who once had tuberculosis could come into this life and get chronic fatigue. Folks who were once affected by some sort of plague can have any number of disruptive illnesses for which there are no current medical names.

So many of you are walking around in this world half alive but completely tired and despondent. You really don't know what it's like to enjoy ultimate happiness and health. Yet it's so simple for you to have both!

❀ ❀ ❀

There have been many people down through history who have touched on some aspect of cell memory, but no one has ever really addressed it as specifically as the Master Teachers on my side have. You can use the information they've shared to fight illness and disease, and you can also use it for depression, or the parts of your mind that you feel aren't acting right.

Do you have to have a medical degree to do this? No, but it would be nice if you had some kind of diagram of what's where in your body, so you'd at least know the difference between your liver and your gallbladder and be able to address them correctly. However, you can give your body this blanket command to encourage ultimate wellness: "No matter what life I'm carrying over these phobias, these feelings of inadequacies, and these undiagnosed or diagnosed illnesses from; let the cell memory be dissipated by the white light of the Holy Spirit that surrounds me. I've learned from it."

If you have a particular problem, try to be as specific as you can when you're addressing your body. So if you're struggling with addiction, state, "If I had a dependency in any past life— whether it was to drugs or alcohol or any other substance—I want to release that morphic resonance and cell memory that's causing my addiction in this life. It does not apply and is not relevant." Or if you have a weight problem, say, "If I had a life in which I starved to death or was constantly hungry, I release the morphic resonance and cell memory that's causing me to overeat in this life. It does not apply and is not relevant." Rinse your cells clean of whatever is causing you problems, since it doesn't need to be there anymore.

When you're thinking of the morphic resonance of your cells, I want you to ask yourself the following every morning for at least a week: "At what age did I feel the best in this life? Was I 7, was I 10, was I 16, or was I 30?" When did you feel the most free and on top of things, surrounded by positive energy? Bring that memory up to the present day and demand that your cells convert themselves to that "happiest" of times and retain the knowledge for everyday operation.

I guarantee that when you do this, people will begin to tell you, "I can't believe what you've done to yourself . . . why do you look so much younger? Why are you so much more vibrant? Why is there a spring in your step?" No matter how many lotions you use or how much exercise you get, it can't compare to what bringing up the best of your cell memory can do for you. I want to stress that if you picked the cell memory of being ten years old, that doesn't mean you're now going to start jumping rope or whatever you did at that age, but you are going to bring the knowledge of that cell memory forward to work for you and your body.

I advise you to use this technique on others, even if they're terminal. For example, Sylvia's currently helping a doctor friend of hers who should be dead by now, at least according to medical science. She's working with him on cell memory, and he's lasting and lasting because he's so open to this positive programming. It's a shame that people have to get to the terminal state before they want to listen to anything that has to do with how to take care of their bodies . . . not that I believe life must be clung to, since true bliss can only be found when you come Home to the Other Side. But while you're attending Earth's "school," you should at least be healthy and happy. Overcoming your cell memory and morphic resonance will accomplish this—after all, if your physiological or mental mechanisms aren't working right, how can *you* possibly feel right?

🍀 🍀 🍀

Research Group Q & A

Q: How does cell memory retain itself?

A: It's sort of like how you automatically start shivering when you get cold: whenever the basic self encounters adversity, it will react until you can stop that reaction. Note that when you're very cold, your muscles contract and your teeth chatter; but if you loosen your muscles, you won't be nearly as cold, and your teeth won't chatter. Similarly, every woman who's given birth knows that if she tenses, the labor pains will be excruciating; if she relaxes and breathes, the pain won't be nearly as bad.

When something stressful or upsetting occurs, it helps to tell yourself, "The worst that can happen just might happen. If it does, I'll take a deep breath and act as if I'm observing it from far away." This neutralizes your worry, as if you shot an arrow right into this dark balloon. To that end, if you have a negative employee, co-worker, spouse, child, or friend—or you're dealing with any unpleasant situation—state, "I'm going to rise above it. I'm going to surround them or the situation with the white light of the Holy Spirit, and I'm not even going to address it."

Cell memory is actually meant for you to face adversity and conquer it by neutralizing it, not necessarily by going in with a sword and making mincemeat of it, but by ignoring the issue as if it didn't exist. This doesn't mean you're hiding your head in the sand; it's just that the more you talk about it, the worse it's going to get. It will be as if you've given life to it, so it becomes bigger and bigger and uglier and uglier.

Say you've gone through an abuse issue: you write about it, you tell other people about it, and they talk back to you about it . . . and pretty soon it becomes a living, breathing monster on its own. Now, does that mean you shouldn't talk about it at all? No, you absolutely should—but then get rid of it. Slay that dragon, and be done with it once and for all.

Q: Will my cells reincarnate with me?

A: No, but there's a memory within your entire molecular structure that seems to come in with you. So if you've had an episode in this life in which you almost drowned at a very early age, don't you think that your whole cell makeup would shudder at the thought of deep water? Of course it would. Compound that with all of the incarnations you've had and the moral or even mental issues that you've gone through—the debasement of self, the possibility that you might have been burned or tortured in a life, the theme of ultimate rejection in so many lives—and you should be very proud that you're even able to stand in an upright position, as Sylvia says.

Q: What can I do to help my body heal from an injury other than talk to it?

A: Sometimes you can talk to an injured part of your body until you're blue in the face and not have any effect. If you've cajoled it, worked with it, and tried to be easy on it, but everything has failed, then your cell memory in that part of the body is basically talking back to you . . . and it's saying no. Perhaps you're just not supposed to be doing a particular type of strenuous physical activity or exercise.

You must always remember that your chart is the ultimate ruler, and sometimes your desire for something will be overruled because you don't see the bigger, overall picture. You may be doing something that's too strenuous or that your body simply can't do in this life. It might be best to stop and try some alternative activities.

Q: Can we help other people with physical handicaps using cell memory?

A: Yes, you can. You must remember, however, that physical handicaps are almost always charted. Everyone comes in with a handicap of some sort—the human body is a handicap in and of itself, even if you have full use of it. But you can all make things in your earthly vehicle so much better by affirming: *I minimize that handicap and bring myself to my ultimate.* God will know what that means, as will your cell memory.

Now, let's take a person who's charted to have an accident and become a quadriplegic. He may never have complete control over his body because he charted it that way, but if he engages his will, he'll be able to do better work and live more productively. He won't totally forget about his physical shell, but he'll be able to adjust and put himself on a higher level.

Q: Why would some great minds choose to be housed in disabled bodies?

A: While you might say, "Oh, the poor things," that's so wrong. These "poor things" are actually very absorbed in their mental work and free of their physical shells. Likewise, some ill people say that they've been "healed" because they've gone into the spirit self and are no longer in the basic self. Individuals are often afraid to ascend to this level because they think that it's only for gurus, those who sit cross-legged on a mountaintop and stare out over the land.

Q: Wouldn't the spirit self help with love?

A: Oh, yes. Normally, cell memory is carried by old wounds, so the least bit of a similar situation can bring back your old response. If you've had a love affair that ended badly, a song might open the wound, causing it to "bleed" down the front of you and "splatter" on everybody else. It's painful! You can heal it by simply saying something to the effect of, "All this is passing. I'm above this."

If you put yourself in the spirit self, it will put you in an almost-timeless place, causing you to heal these painful wounds once and for all. Did you ever notice that when you're having a good time, the hours fly by? When you're having a bad time, on the other hand, the hours creep by at a snail's pace. If you have a bad day at work or aren't busy, every time you look at the clock, it seems that only three minutes have passed.

You see, your mind can get stuck on something, such as the unrequited love that you see so much of in the world, or the "I want to find my soul mate" syndrome. Men and women wander through life looking for their perfect mate, never realizing for one moment that *they're* not perfect! They're spending a useless, lonely, pining-away life feeling that they're never going to have a partner, when there can be so many individuals they can partner with—not only friends and loved ones, but those who really need care as well, such as children or the elderly. Most people are screaming, "Please give me a body to sleep with!" never realizing that they have to sleep with themselves. Folks must realize that they should be tremendously in love with *themselves* and the other half of themselves—that is, both the male and female parts.

Instead of worrying and obsessing about romance, you can rise above it into the spirit self and get on with your life. And chances are that once this happens, you'll find a wonderful person to love because you won't be so frantic about it.

Q: If something upsets us emotionally, are we able to rinse that out?

A: Of course! Just say, "Whatever morphic resonance I'm responding to, let it be released." Let's say you were persecuted in a past life because of your religious beliefs, and then this feeling of being unloved or unwanted now comes up because of a broken relationship. If you smite the morphic resonance of persecution in a past life, you'll be able to deal with rejection better in this one.

Q: Is it important to know the time that caused the morphic resonance?

A: It's not important. In fact, too much of this going back and digging things up isn't useful. I think that's why I've always felt that regressive therapy is so good: it neutralizes; it puts you into an objective position; and after you live through it somewhat, you release it. I don't think that you have to go back and dredge everything up to be free of it. Your mind is such a marvelous mechanism that it will respond to what you demand.

Q: I've suffered abuse all my life. Did that happen to me in a past life?

A: Yes, you were practically kept as a hostage by your father in a place in France. You were very attractive, but he never let you date, never let you go outside, and never let you be with people . . . and he sexually abused you. The cell memory of your soul only knows pain, and unfortunately, it will seek out more pain because it's so familiar. You can change that by vehemently protesting, "I don't deserve this, and I won't accept it! I'll reject and eject anything that doesn't illuminate my soul to its greatest ability." You aren't going to interfere with your soul's learning if you do this—enough is enough!

Q: Can mental abuse affect us physically?

A: On my side, we find that mental abuse is actually worse on the soul than physical or even sexual abuse is—not that I'm for any type of abuse, but we see the scar appear on the soul from mental abuse. While put-downs like, "You're stupid, you're ugly, you're dumb, and you're not good for anything" primarily scar the soul, the effects of mental abuse do indeed show on the body as well.

Individuals who have been abused can have a hard time losing weight, or else they lose too much. They have a problem with their eyes because they've seen too much. They have problems with their hearing because they've heard too much. They have a problem with their heart because it's been broken. They have a problem with their back because that's where they've carried everything. They have problems with their knees because the abuse has made them bow. There is a literal factor that happens with the physical body, and it screams all the time about what's wrong . . . yet no one will listen.

When it comes to any type of abuse from any life, just release it on a blanket command.

Q: Can cell memory come from people we've seen in other lives?

A: Cell memory goes into such a wide scope: your soul recognizes other souls from the past, along with places and experiences both good and bad. You'll resonate to certain beliefs such as Gnosticism, Mormonism, Catholicism, or whatever. You'll resonate to certain countries, cultures, or

lifestyles. And you can even resonate to certain structures like the Taj Mahal or the pyramids. All of life is a
resonance.

Q: How much of my health problems are due to past-life cell memory?

A: To find out the answer to this, try to track back and
address what in your family or your own structure could
have caused your health problems . . . they're not all due
to past lives. I'd say that a majority of health problems are
actually the result of patterns in your current incarnation,
and if you know that certain patterns are responsible
for your illness, you can break them. If you tend to get
migraines at a certain time of the month, for instance,
track to see what happens in your life just before you
get that headache. It might be that you have to give a
monthly report to your boss, and the stress of that event
brings on the pain.

Q: How do we know if it was a past life creating a health problem or something we charted for the present?

A: It doesn't really matter. When you get an infection,
very few doctors ask you how you got it, do they? They
just treat you. (Of course what they ought to do is track
the cause because you have so many strange illnesses
coming to Earth now.)

I'd just address your body with a blanket command to cover all factors: "If I'm bringing over this pain or illness from a past life when I incurred some trauma or injury, or if it's something I've experienced in this life, release it!" Tell the cell memory to get rid of it and order the natural defense mechanisms of the body to attack any virus or infection or bad cells.

Q: What's the correct way to reach cell memory in regressions?

A: People are afraid of verbal usage and try to mask it in terms that they think are more understandable or tactful. It's best to just be direct and tell your subject's body, "We're now going to address morphic resonance and cell memory. Whatever negativity we've carried over from any time will be released. We're now going to bring up the spirit self; we're going to have it devoid of any and all appendages that are holding you back, whether it was from mental, spiritual, or physical afflictions. Whatever seed was planted from whatever time it came, give me the scenario when this first began to root."

Let's say you're helping an alcoholic. Start by asking him, "What precipitated the first drink you ever took? Was it to show off? Was it to be part of the gang?"

Suppose he answers, "I was 13 years old, and a friend of mine got killed in an accident." Don't leave it at that; take him further back by inquiring, "When did you first began to drink in another life, and why?" (I don't mean to imply that anything is wrong with alcohol; I'm addressing alcoholism here.)

He might reply, "I was in a pub in Ireland after my mother died. I was all alone, and I began to drink." All right, now we're getting somewhere . . . do you see how the pattern is repeating?

Ask your subject, "Do you think that there's any connection between your being in a pub after losing your mother in a past life and being 13 and losing a friend in this life—both events that started you drinking?" See what I'm saying? Once you begin to pull up the weed, it has a tremendous healing effect.

Time is circular, and knowing this helps healing. As you move through this circuitous time, you can go back and clean up any part of the journey. This also addresses cell memory, along with the memory from this life and transplant memory. You can in fact do "surgery" on yourself—get rid of the bad portions of the body by "transplanting" the good parts of yourself that come from previous lives. You won't really use any other organs, but let's say that your organs from a past time were working for you. You can take yourself back to a time in this life in which you were at optimal health and even get rid of all the seeds of congenital or inherited illnesses.

Q: When we're healing others, do we have to go back to a specific life to grab cell memory?

A: No. I'd actually address *this* life by asking, "When was the first time you began to feel that arthritic pain? What precipitated that? What happened a week, two weeks, and a month right before that?"

You may hear something like, "Oh, nothing much . . . except my husband divorced me." This person can't make the conscious connection that the rigidity in her body could come from being rejected unless it's pointed out to her or she does some investigating on her own.

Q: Did we write morphic resonance into our chart to help us fine-tune a lesson from a past life?

A: Oh sure, you make it appear in your chart when you need it. Many times you go over and over the same thing, and guess what? You'll ultimately learn from it. No one, not in any life, is smart enough to comprehend everything in just one incarnation. You have to just keep going through it until you finally get it.

Q: Do we get more phobias and anxieties with more lives?

A: It turns out that the more lives you've had, the more phobic you could indeed become. I know that's not exactly a selling point for more lives, but what happens is that a person who's taken on a lot of incarnations finds that everything condenses on the last life. As most people on Earth are now on their last lives, all of these morphic resonances come forward at once, so we're seeing more and more men and women with phobias and anxieties.

Q: Francine, have you had any personal experience with cell memory?

A: My life in 1500 was certainly not pleasant. You may think it was simplistic, but it wasn't. I was impaled by a spear and died very young—and I elected not to come back, but to be a guide instead. Yet I'm sure that if I were to come back into a life again, I'd have a very definite problem with my chest area. This brings up something else: working out your preordained karmic experience, whether you do so on your side or mine . . . there's no way to escape that. I actually find it very comforting to know that I'll perfect, even sometimes against my own will, and you shall, too.

❀ ❀ ❀   ❀ ❀ ❀

Chapter 13

Getting in Touch with Your True Essence

Francine: On my side, we know that the human soul gathers information from life after life and carries with it all types of mannerisms, phobias, and aesthetic values. The thing that's most important is: *in no way is your essence ever disturbed.* You as an entity—with all of your personality and depth, along with the things you've learned over the course of your entire existence—stay the same. The more you stick to the essence of you, the less you'll be attacked or have illnesses or problems . . . and the more life will deal with you gently.

There is a universal truth that's a guiding light for you all, and that's to simplify your life as much as possible by getting in touch with that essential you, or your spirit self. By no means does this go against the idea that you can have material gain, that you can be successful, that you can have a wonderful relationship, or that you can have some contentment of soul. However, wanting things too much sends your soul into a "wobble" that can throw you off track. Have you ever thought about your desires compared to someone who lives in the Sudan? That person's solitary thought for the day is, *Please let me find food and water.* It's all about survival.

You might say, "Francine, we're in a world of commercialism, so we need our homes and cars." Of course you do, and there's nothing wrong with that. In no way do I want this to seem like a communistic approach, because the one thing that has kept all souls free is the democracy of enterprise in any form. But if you go to the level of your spirit self, you'll realize that the things you tend to want in life are transitory. Of course you need water, food, shelter, *and* love . . . that's part of the plan of God. Where you fall into a pit of despair—where the morphic resonance or cell memory seems to come back and bite you—is when you become so desirous of things that are so far beyond those basic needs. So learn to rein yourself in by affirming, *I have enough of all that I require, along with a great deal of contentment.*

By doing this, you'll be following in Christ's footsteps. Now, when Jesus asked people to follow him, he didn't mean that they had to give up their worldly possessions. He was really asking, "Do you have enough courage to drop everything else that you've been taught and follow the simple path I'm showing you? Let's walk, let's talk, and let's be together. Let's eat, let's drink, and let's find a place for the night." And his followers did.

You must realize that the Jesus Christ who walked the world was a wealthy man, much like Siddhartha (the Buddha). I don't care if you've been told that Jesus was a poor carpenter; that's a lie. His father was a very well-known, well-to-do businessman who did custom furnishings—a fact that's borne out in the scriptures when the Roman soldiers cast lots over Christ's garments when he was crucified. Only the wealthy had such garments, which had to be transported over a long distance by caravan. Jesus may have been given his clothes, but they certainly wouldn't have been given to someone not of the elitist rank. Such garments would never have been donated to some scruffy beggar walking around with this group of ragtag men who were wandering over the fields spouting all kinds of dissident philosophies.

So I'm not saying that you should give up your home, clothes, jewelry, or car—I'm saying you are too tied in to them, however, and have been this way for so many eons of time. The problem is that most entities don't address the basic self before they get to their desires, and that's where the wobble comes in. This is why Jesus made a very definite directive to "love yourself." When you love yourself, you ultimately rule out a lot of the garbage you've carried with you from life after life that's so encumbering. You stop giving credence to the negative views of life, such as "I'll be sued," "I'll be put through terrible anguish," "I'll be rejected," "I'll be neglected," "I'll be abandoned," and other powerless beliefs.

Many psychologists have called the basic self "the child within," and there have been all types of terms for, and theories about, humans' primal, instinctual nature. I think the basic self is actually responsible for the ancient view that humanity is animalistic and even putrid. Well, the basic self is not putrid, but it does drive you to eat, sleep, procreate, and survive . . . it also pushes you to achieve. Thus, it can become obsessive and compulsive, keeping the spirit self from getting through.

You must be very hard on the basic self because it comes in with all these morphic resonances that cause you to focus on worries such as *What if I get fired? What if all my money is wiped out? What if I lose all that I've gained? What if I can't take care of my family? What if I have to let everybody down?* I'd be willing to bet that most of you have had these fears at one time or another, along with thoughts such as *I'm alone, I'm distraught, I'm abandoned, I'm rejected, I'm victimized,* and *God is unfair.*

These concerns bring you to a point where no light can come in. In order to get your basic self up to reach your spirit self and get rid of some of these silly, phobic, and reactionary feelings about your life—regarding your relationships, your weight, what's going to happen with the stock market, and so forth—know that you're going to live, you're going to have some joy, you're going to have some sorrow, and then you're going to return to the Other Side. That's the greatest truth you'll know.

You must accept that life on Earth is simply negative and much like a minefield. You can be so cautious that you never even attempt to go through it, or you can take the chance of venturing forth and possibly stepping on a mine. It's certainly better to make your way through the field instead of standing there trembling and never moving forward. If you blow up, is that the worst thing that can happen to you? You might protest, "But I'd be ruined!" How so? Your soul can't be ruined. How horrible would it be if you died? That isn't horrible . . . it means that you get to go Home.

☙ ☙ ☙

As difficult as this may be for you to understand, your brain is always in a state of rejecting the human form. That's because being in a body is not where your true self needs or likes to be; it's in a place where it has to be to gain perfection. You're taking your magnificent soul and pushing it into a physiological mechanism that doesn't fit well. The more advanced the soul becomes, the less it fits with the body.

Here's something you can say that's so easy and simple you won't believe it can work . . . until you start doing it and seeing the rapid results. Just state, "I'm not *of* my body; I'm *above* it. I don't reside in my body at all." Of course this doesn't mean you're supposed to rule out pain or anything that's a valid signal that you should take care of your body. I wouldn't expect you to drive a car with faulty brakes or a transmission that didn't operate right. But I *would* expect you to take care of the person in the car more than you take care of the vehicle, because the person is going to survive. Whereas the car will get old, rust, and break down; the soul never does. The soul is eternal, and it's loved and protected by God.

The soul is always fighting with your basic self—the self that has been burned, crucified, shot, strangled, raped, pillaged, or plundered throughout your lifetimes—and it can become very depressed in the process. Yet you can help your soul rise above this condition by stating in your own words that not only are you going to get rid of the morphic resonance of your existence, but you're going to pull your energy and your mind from your lower basic self into the high-mindedness of the spirit self as well.

I know I've addressed the right and left brain many times, but I'd like to do so again. It's most helpful to cement the two halves of yourself—your emotion and your intellect—together by asking God

172

to marry them. You can then tell your body not to allow your basic self to take over, just as you wouldn't let your intellect or emotion take over one side of your brain or the other.

Living in a Negative World

You reside on a planet in which other people are always giving out statements of doom and gloom—they'll walk up to you and announce how tired you look or how overworked you are. This may be their way of expressing concern for you, but don't accept anything negative! Just walk away and silently say to yourself, "Cancel that!"

Since the world is being ruled by negativity, it creates a situation in which you're constantly under psychic attack. Psychic attacks don't come from a demon, but from the darkness of the world—crime, terrorism, wars, natural disasters, and the like. They can also come from the men and women around you: you're told that you're unworthy, you're no good, you're a bad mother or father, you can't hold a job, and on and on it goes. It's like you're listening to a recording of a constant barrage of negativity . . . and how you react to it determines your spiritual growth and soul's learning process.

The best way to fight it is to tell that recording, "Enough! I will not be programmed, and I will not let it affect me!" Negativity only builds upon negativity, particularly on the hellish planet that is Earth. But even as you witness its horrors, you can keep yourself from being touched by them in a way that reduces their impact to wear you down. So if you want to watch the news, for instance, then do so as objectively as you can. You don't need to keep yourself in a bubble, but with things that you can do nothing about, say, "I reject that. At the same time, I'll do as much good as I possibly can in the circle I'm in."

All challenging individuals and things are actually in God's plan to make souls perfect. You have to understand that although darkness is ruling the globe, humanity is in fact being led into the light. Unfortunately, there have to be a lot of sacrificial lambs along the way, so when you see a great leader assassinated, know that he or she chose that. You might wonder, "Why would anybody choose to go that way?" For the greater good! Otherwise, you're left with random acts—and as Sylvia has said, God is not playing Russian roulette with everyone's lives.

Be careful of always thinking that you know best. Otherwise, you're beating your head against a wall as you try to make people do what you want them to. It never works, does it? It's great to attempt to help and do good for others, but don't insist that they do what's really best for you. Just try to do good works and deal with others in the most positive way possible, and let them live their own lives according to their charts.

As Jesus said, don't drop your pearls in front of swine. Don't stay in relationships that are miserable for you, since you won't accomplish any karmic debt except to yourself. Karma is the law of cause and effect; that is, everything you put out comes back to you. It truly is the reaping of what you sow. Now that doesn't mean that every time you get mad at someone, someone will get mad at you. And if you have righteous anger, such as for a cause, that won't come back to you. As Sylvia has said, it's all in the motive.

If you have a disruptive person in your life, ask for the Holy Spirit to neutralize and cut him or her off from you. This saves you from continually being dependent on the happiness of another— after all, there's no happiness in this world more important than your own. You might say, "That's selfish." No, it isn't. By bringing yourself the truest joy that you can have, you'll find that you can then share it with someone else.

❖ ❖ ❖

There are so many things that we guides who are protecting you see you battle. We perceive the negativity that surrounds you and all the things that you cannot control in your life—you should at least be in charge of your body. Get up in the morning and do a cleansing by saying, "Whatever is in my cell memory, let it be dissipated by the white light of the Holy Spirit that surrounds me. I have learned from it." You don't need to be phobic or disturbed on top of everything else. After all, even though you've charted your way, why wouldn't you want to stay as happy and healthy as possible as you go through what you've written in for yourself?

Now, I have been very much for Western medicine, as Sylvia is, but I'm also into alternative and holistic treatments. I think that in your lifetime, you'll eventually see science and spirituality meld together. Religion will not be part of this, however, since it has always been at loggerheads with science, and rightfully so. But thanks to the quantum leap of spirituality, science will get on the spiritual bandwagon because it does go into all the laws of relativity.

I'm not asking that you negate your personal faith, but you should definitely augment the prayers you've learned with your own. You can say a prayer so often that you end up just giving lip service to it. Most of you have recited the Lord's Prayer so many times, for instance, that you don't even realize what you're saying anymore. Coming up with your own prayers makes things much more powerful and personal because you're talking to your Creator from your own heart and soul. You don't even have to pray per se—you can simply have a conversation with your God and discuss what's going on in your life and how to solve any problems you might have.

The more simplistic prayers are, the more they touch your true essence. This brings up your awareness because you aren't just reaching the God without; you're reaching the God within, which certainly requires protection and solace. Also, be sure to visualize or ask for your glorified body to descend upon you. Your glorified body is what you assume when you die and go through the tunnel to the Other Side—it's your spirit self, the perfect you. The more you aspire to being like the glorified body, the more it begins to descend upon you, and what you really are unfolds to the outside.

༺ ༺ ༺

You can stand in front of a mirror all day and say, "In every way I'm getting better and better," but this isn't specific enough, nor does it get you to the core of things. Take it one step further and affirm: *I am a well person in a well body, and I am also geared for success.* This is the true form of programming.

Although you won't be able to stop the aging process—because you really don't want to—this positive programming will keep you young longer. It's so silly that anyone would believe the message your society sends that after a certain age, human beings should no longer do things. When I lived my only life in the Aztec-Inca community, even though I died very young, there were men and women in our village who were 93 or 94 years of age, and this was in the 1500s. No one told them they weren't supposed to carry big grain baskets or go out in the fields—the philosophy we all believed was that we worked until we died, and we'd be fit throughout our lives. Our elders might walk a little slower, but they'd still get the job done. Because that programming was there, nobody thought about saying, "You're too old to work."

Human beings are supposed to be on their feet until they drop—they're not supposed to be cradled in a bed or wheelchair. Do you realize that until rather recently, there was no such thing as a wheelchair? If folks had some deficiency in their legs, they were carried. In my village, for instance, the strongest men carried our loved ones who were disabled wherever they wanted to go. You might think that would be hard on people, but I think it's worse to put someone in a steel contraption where everybody stares at them. If you see somebody being carried, that is a kind, loving act.

༺ ༺ ༺

RESEARCH GROUP Q & A

Q: Please tell us more about the glorified body. It's the same as the spirit self?

A: Yes. When you go through the tunnel to the Other Side upon death, you begin to absorb your perfect self: it doesn't have any illnesses, hidden agendas, problems, phobias, crises, or pain; and it only contains your true spirit. All of the negativity drops away, and you feel light as a feather and absolutely marvelous, which is why death is such a painless and wonderful experience (besides the fact that you're going Home).

On the Other Side, we're all 30 years of age. We're very discernible to each other, but we don't have the same visage. We very likely take on an appearance we had in some life that we dearly loved. People have asked so many times over the years, "How will I know my loved ones if they look different than when I knew them?" Well, when you're on the Other Side, your mind is opened up to its full capacity, and soul recognizes soul. Entities can have visages in any size, shape, or color; but souls will always recognize each other because of our Home's advanced state of awareness.

Q: We should ask for our glorified body to exude our essence into our current form?

A: Right. You already have it within you, so you can ask it to spring forth at any time. You don't realize how much you carry within yourself—you have no idea what kind of power you have within you. It really is the essence of the individual that can pull itself out and morph itself into this glorified being. Morphic resonances come out of you; cell memory comes out of you; the glorified body comes out of you. You don't even realize what a "package" you're carrying.

Q: Is this like the ancient Chinese "chi" or life force, wherein your power is greater than anything physical you may do?

A: Absolutely, it's one and the same. A point I keep coming back to (because I watched it firsthand) was when Sylvia once mistakenly grabbed a hot poker and immediately screamed "No!" The vehemence of the *No!* inside of her mind was so strong that every part of the essence of her glorified body reacted and she wasn't burned or hurt in any way.

Q: Can we develop our chi to flush our cells?

A: Oh, sure. You can also use any exercise that gets your heart rate up to flush yourself and bring about the whole morphic resonance of the total, complete chi . . . the glorified body.

Q: Is the glorified body the same as the oversoul?

A: Yes, they're one and the same—different religions or philosophies just have different names for the same thing. You must realize that it all refers to your spirit self, your true essence that actually resides outside of your earthly body, although you're not aware of it.

Q: So the key is to get into the spirit self outside of the body in order to conquer the basic self?

A: That's right. On my side, we know that before you come in to life on Earth, you have every intention of whipping this basic human self into shape. That self has to be there, for without it you wouldn't experience any of life's trials or tribulations and learn from them. The problem is when you go overboard and allow negative programming to almost take on a life of its own. You start to become paranoid, convinced that *They're out to get me* or *The world is cruel.* If you live in the spirit self, the world isn't nearly so cruel or frightening—you know that it will never show you very much that you can't get through.

Does becoming more spiritual take years and years of sitting cross-legged somewhere with a guru? No. You can go ahead and shop, get your hair done, play some golf, open a restaurant, or do all the wondrous things human beings like to do in the process.

Q: How does the glorified body affect our immune system?

A: Your perfect self has complete immunity to everything, so the more you get into that glorified body, the more your immunity goes up and self-healing takes place. What causes illness is honestly that you're too much in your physical shell. *Be above the body*—I can't stress that to you enough. The more you remove yourself from the body, the better you'll feel, and your immunity will skyrocket.

Q: Can addressing the primitive brain help?

A: Since morphic resonance is stored in the primitive (limbic) brain and many healing methods utilize it, you should absolutely address it.

Have you ever noticed how when people are really happy or in great pain, they yell everything out? Exclaiming "God help me!" or "God, I'm so happy!" helps them ventilate their pain or share their joy. This is what you should do, too. Who cares if you go in the bathroom and scream, "Get this morphic resonance off of me!"? You don't have to shout so that everybody upstairs, downstairs, or to the side of you hears; just vehemently state: "Let my glorified body come out! Let the cell memory dissolve!"

I'd like to see you do this for your entire life, but if you only do it for a solid week, you'll still see definite results. Other people will start asking you, "What have you been doing to yourself? Did you get a face-lift? Have you lost weight? Have you gotten more rest?" They won't know how to pinpoint it, but they'll definitely note that something's happening—they'll witness the light shining from you, the chrysalis shedding, and the butterfly emerging. You're forcing those layers to go away . . . think of it as a chemical peel for your body and mind that isn't painful in any way.

On my side, we find that you on Earth are so afraid to release your pain or your agendas. You don't want to let go and be naked, stripped of those layers of fat, scars, or hurt. It's easy to hold on to those things—once they're gone, a level of your mind won't know what to do. Sometimes people are identified by their pain, their scars, their weight, or even their thinness. You take that away from them and suddenly they feel terribly fragile and vulnerable because their friend is gone. But just like when Sylvia yelled "No!" as she picked up the poker and removed herself from the reality of that moment, you can change the molecular structure of the reality. You can in fact step outside of time.

Q: Will we be negating time or physical things?

A: It doesn't matter because it's the same—you're vibrating and changing matter. When you go into your glorified body, you're at a higher frequency, and nothing on this lower level of matter has anything to do with it. You perceive things differently and begin to take the overview by letting go of the false ego. It's like Sylvia says, "You walk the walk; you talk the talk."

Q: **Stuff won't bother us as much?**

A: Exactly. The petty things of the world fall away: the things that would have irritated you before no longer do; your magnanimous feelings go beyond that. The people who live downstairs and have drunken parties every Friday night, which used to drive you crazy . . . you won't even hear them anymore.

Q: **How can we stay above our body at the highest vibration possible and flow with life?**

A: Many times during the day, simply affirm: *I am not in the body.* You see, if you are in the body, it becomes heavy and gross—you won't flow with life, and things bother you more.

Q: **Is it possible to increase our intelligence?**

A: Absolutely. State: "For an hour or two, I want to detach from the basic self."

For total comprehension of this concept, suppose that you're completely absorbed in something such as a good book. I'm sure you weren't thinking, *I'm lying on the bed with the light on, I have this book in my hand, and my feet are in a certain position*—you were totally immersed in the reality of that book.

Or think about children, who become so totally engrossed by things that when you're calling to them, they often don't hear you. You almost have to get up in front of their face and wave your hand to get their attention. You as adults tend to lose that focus, but the more you can get it back, the better it will be for you. Meditation and mantras help train you to become absorbed—even if you're just staring at a dot, you become that dot. This causes your basic self to become quiet and fade, and that's when your spirit self takes over and elevates your mind.

We always hear, "People don't know how to study; they have poor learning habits." That's so wrong. They're never been taught how to *focus* or become totally engaged by something.

Now, it might take any number of pursuits or activities to get you to that point, but keep trying: whether it's looking at works of art in a museum, gazing out at the ocean, or reading a good book, practice being absorbed. Anything that totally engrosses you will release the basic self, causing the spirit self to rise! It doesn't have to be an intellectual pursuit, but it should be a thing of beauty because that elevates your mind anyway. Each time you do this activity, it will push the lower self down, but it will also increase your mental acuity.

Q: Can our desires take us off track from our charts?

A: Oh, yes. It's like you have a strong urge to go through a door, but every time you do, you cut yourself. How many times would you need to go through that door to learn that you're not meant to go through it? Understand that while you might not be able to go through that door, there will always be a window or other opening for you to use.

For example, you may have a knee injury that doesn't allow you to participate in a physical activity such as a very challenging martial art. While you may not be able to do that particular martial art, you may be able to do a gentler form of it. That is, you don't have to stop your practice . . . but you should modify it.

The basic self is the protectorate, and it will set up all kinds of warnings when you're veering off course. When Sylvia got blood poisoning in her foot, for instance, she asked me, "What is this about?" I replied, "Well, you just would not listen when I told you that you've been working too hard and running too fast. The only way to stop you was to do this to you." Needless to say, she wasn't too happy about it, but she healed just fine (and it did slow her down for a time).

Q: So we shouldn't want things in life?

A: Once you've gotten rid of your past behavioral overlays with your meditation or self-hypnosis, you can certainly ask for wealth and prosperity to shine upon you. *Prosperity* is a word that encompasses more than wealth—it means to be prosperous in friends, as well as to rise up to your full potential. Never be afraid to ask for abundance! As Sylvia likes to say, "If God didn't want you to have it, He wouldn't have put it here for you to aspire to." So ask for abundance to come and for miracles to happen. Program yourself for whatever you desire and want to accomplish . . . it will help you obtain it if you've already chosen it for yourself in your chart.

Q: If we heal others, do we intercept their charts?

A: No. In fact, you should assume that you were written into their charts to cure or alleviate their pain. Who's to say you weren't meant to help them? Nothing is by accident! The fact that you came in contact with those who needed help shows that in all probability, you were meant to help them in any way you could. Sylvia struggled with that for a long time—she thought that by doing readings, she was interfering with people's charts and intercepting what they'd written for themselves. No, Sylvia Browne was written into their charts, the same as anyone else who could help them was.

Yes, there are some people who cannot or will not be helped because that's what they've written in their charts, but don't assume that. You have to approach each healing as if it will be successful and let God's will (and the will of the person being healed) be done.

❀ ❀ ❀   ❀ ❀ ❀

Chapter 14

Meditations for Healing

(**Important note from Sylvia:** This chapter contains meditations. Now, anybody can meditate, and the practice may be done in any position that you're comfortable with, be it sitting, lying down, or whatever. In any meditation, however, it's best to close your eyes and make your body as relaxed as possible by loosening up all of your muscles from head to toe before you start. It is also advisable that if you like a particular meditation, you make a recording of it with your own voice—then when you're ready, you can simply play it and let it lead you through the steps.)

Francine: I'd like to address the archetypal symbol of the star that you've brought into life with you, just as you've brought certain phobias. On my side, we know that every human being incarnates with a fear of falling, for example. But the primordial fear that's so deeply seated in every entity comes from trying to find a sense of belonging.

Your basic self causes that phobic reaction of being set adrift or going away to school (which is what life on Earth is). I'm not sure that you can ever overcome this feeling of alienation until you encompass the totality of what you're going back to, completely understanding that your Home resides on the Other Side. The fear of annihilation or death can come from not knowing that you do go to a place that's far more beautiful and full of more ecstasy and bliss than this earthly plane will ever know.

When dealing with phobias, you should be proud of yourself that you've gotten this far in your lifetime, regardless of what age you are. You do come in as a child in a little body, even though your soul is big. For any child to be put in alien surroundings (even though you've chosen parents) and be able to survive is extraordinary. It's like you can read all the travelogues and plan your trip, but that's not the same as actually going. Sometimes even the best-laid plans are interrupted because other charts intercept yours and things can become delayed or derailed—not for any length of time for those who walk in the light, but derailed nonetheless.

So when you incarnate, you walk around feeling lost: you feel that you've lost your homeland, your true identity, and your loved ones; you're also sure that you've lost the pure knowledge you had that was all-encompassing, from every life you lived. You're set adrift on a foreign shore with people who speak a different language than you do, with a body that stops you from ever being able to totally merge with another human being. You wonder why the morphic resonance of your soul doesn't rebel . . . well, of course it does. It rebels through human illness—through cancer, arthritis, ulcers, obesity, and myriad other afflictions.

In many ways, your soul is constantly hoping that you'll eventually get something that will send you Home, which sets up a dichotomy within the human form. You were meant to come down and learn, but there's another side of you that really doesn't know why you're here until you make that grand journey back—not necessarily to the Other Side, but back to your true self.

You discover what you're here to learn, which brings you some sort of peace. That's when the fear of death, of annihilation, and even of homesickness for the Other Side begins to diminish. When you finally understand that this is only a temporal plane of existence and you'll soon be Home, that knowledge permeates every fiber of your being and gives you the strength to survive. It's like being given a release date after a long prison sentence. Just knowing the date you'll be free helps you hang in there until you can be with all your friends and family members again.

Life, in fact, can be likened to a cell in two ways. Not only is your body constructed of cells, but it's like a jail because your soul is imprisoned in flesh. And when you stop and think about all of the morphic resonance that you've carried from life after life, it can really be overwhelming.

❀ ❀ ❀

Whether it has four, five, or six points, the star has had great importance throughout history. It's such a powerful symbol that it figures prominently in the Judaic and Islamic faiths; it's also what is supposed to shine when any messiah is born. And the star has long appeared in literature, as well as the ancient lore of mythology.

So now I'd like to give you a wonderful tool to use called "the Star Treatment." While it may sound esoteric, it's really very effective. This isn't a technique to be used for protection but rather for healing and the relief of pain. When it comes to protection, imagine that you're using a silver net, which is a protective device like the white light of the Holy Spirit or mirrors that surround you and face outward. You see a net of silver completely surrounding you and it repels negativity and evil . . . but it should be used very judiciously.

If you have an undiagnosed malady, or it's been diagnosed but you can't seem to get any relief, then you're a prime candidate for the Star Treatment. Now, this technique involves the use of the mind and its ability to visualize, so for those of you who don't think you can do this, here's a quick primer on the subject. First of all, visualization is nothing more than memory or knowledge acquired—you can't visualize something that you've never seen or known anything about. Visualization takes place in your mind, and it's the easiest thing for anyone to do . . . even blind people. For example, if you think of your mother, the memory of how she looks forms inside your mind and becomes a picture; that's visualization. See how simple it is?

To begin this technique, sit or lie down on a bed or couch. You may want to do this at night when it's the most quiet—and you typically see stars shine—but you can practice it at any time.

Relax, close your eyes, and start to visualize a star. The star can have any number of points to it, but do see it as silver blue in color. Watch the star become radiant and pulsate with light . . . make it as radiant and bright as possible, even to the point that you think it might hurt your eyes in its brightness (it will not).

Now that you have this bright, pulsating, silver blue star in your mind's eye, go to any area of your body that needs healing or pain relief, and slap it on the affected area. Use this silver blue star in the quiet night on your stomach, back, head, or whatever area of your body that needs healing. Do make sure that it is in proportion to the area you are dealing with; do not just put a great big star over your whole body but make it localized. It is very much like a cortisone shot or a laser—you want to put it in the place that is giving you the most agony.

Ask your spirit guides to help direct you; if you are having problems with numbness in your hand, for instance, they might tell you to put the star on the back of your neck instead of on the hand itself. Or ask them to lead you, in your mind's eye, and take your first impression. I want you to start getting more reciprocation from your guides and letting them come in.

Once you have the star in the area that needs healing or pain relief, keep visualizing it there: silver blue, pulsating with a bright light of power. I guarantee that as you lie there quietly, you will never feel anything that pulsates like this. When it begins to do so, please do not be frightened. The star, which has been an ancient symbol, is like a doorway to the light, and that light is

*helping heal and relieve your pain . . . causing you to feel better
than you ever have before.*

*When you are ready, bring yourself up, all the way up to
full consciousness, feeling absolutely marvelous. On the count
of three, come all the way up: one, two, three.*

The Star Treatment can also be used for mental acuity as well
as calming anxiety. In your meditation, just place the star right
between your eyes. Or if you're having a problem with your knee,
you could place a star on it, making sure that it wraps around and
encompasses the entire knee. For the heart area, make the star large
enough that it contains the entire region, since it helps to get rid of
all of the problems in the arteries surrounding the heart as well.

The Star Treatment is probably the most powerful visualization
you can use. I haven't shared it before because I don't want it used
lightly; that is, I don't want you to go to bed at night and use it for
any old reason. Yet don't get overly scrupulous about it by saying,
"Oh, I shouldn't have used the Star Treatment just for a headache."
If it's pain to you, then it's pain . . . and for agonizing headaches,
try using a small star over your eye (or both eyes) or sinuses.

You can actually use a number of stars, but do make sure that
you name them. In other words, state: "This is for my elbow, this
is for my shoulder, this is for my chin or my jaw," and so on. You
can put multiple stars on multiple parts of the body at the same
time, or you can make a star and put it on an area and then make
another star and put it on a different area.

✆ ✆ ✆

RESEARCH GROUP Q & A

Q: Can we do the Star Treatment in the morning?

A: You can, to give yourself energy. While you can use it at any time, I always think it's better at night because humans relate to stars as phenomena of the night.

Q: We can use any type of star, even pentagrams?

A: Yes. The mythologies of the ancient Greeks and Romans always looked to the stars as symbols of heavenly intervention, and now you're going to use them in that very way. When you bring the stars down out of the sky and place them on you, you'll find that, if used with the right motive, your basic self will resonate to your spirit self, and it will seem as if they're sealed together.

Since the Star Treatment's silver blue light can burn out illness, let's call it "the Other Side's laser." Other guides have told me that some of their people who used it have gotten rid of all kinds of problems with their body—including tumors. These individuals went to see their doctors, who were astounded by the miraculous turn of events. I don't want to get your hopes up, but I just know how powerful this technique can be (along with seeing your doctor, of course).

Q: How long should we leave the star on?

A: You could leave it on for ten or fifteen minutes—if you can't, then just do it for five. You'll find that the longer you leave it on, the more power it gets. Don't be afraid if you begin to heat up with this technique because there's no way it's going to hurt any of your organs.

Q: What if you put it on and fall asleep?

A: Oh, it's all right—the light goes out. You won't get harmed in any way.

Q: Why make the star silver blue in color?

A: Well, I think it comes from Mother God, as part of Her colors that She resonates to. She also resonates to gold, but more than any other color in the universe, silver blue carries healing with it. You may have heard that green is the healing color, and it should indeed always be used for people who treat and help others—they should visualize the emerald green light all down the front of their body.

But when you really want extra power, use silver blue. From time to time on my side, we've noticed a silver blue light sweeping the earth. We believe that it's emanating from the hands of Mother God and carries a lot of power.

Q: Can we use the Star Treatment for symptoms of illness as well as pain?

A: Absolutely! As you begin to master this technique, you might place the star on your cheek and for some reason feel it pulling to your throat . . . if that happens, let it go where it wants. You may ask, "Why would the star be moving?" It's because your guide is pushing it where it really needs to go.

Q: Would this help after a serious operation?

A: Oh, yes. It would be wonderful because it takes away pain and also helps in the healing process.

Q: What if the illness is in our chart?

A: You can minimize it by using the Star Treatment. Lupus can be helped, sciatica can be helped, or cancer can be helped. You've got to realize you've also written in your chart that you got this information to do something about it. For those reading this book, for instance, you wrote in your chart to receive all the knowledge that Raheim, Sylvia, and I have been sharing with you.

Q: Is the technique to be used on only one area at a time?

A: No, you can use it on multiple areas. But if you're going to do this, be sure to do all the areas at one time. It's best to only use the Star Treatment three times a week—doing it every night won't have the same impact. Other guides and I have noticed that the treatment carries great energy, but when it isn't used so much, it carries more for some reason. So maybe some kind of a recharging factor happens with it. We've also found that people who use it a lot become so euphoric that it's almost like trying to get them off of a drug.

While you can use this treatment for extreme tiredness, it's sort of like one of those elixirs that you want to save for when you really need it. Not that it doesn't have power—and I know I'm confusing you here, but I don't mean to. I'm just saying that anything so blessed should be used sparingly, or only when needed.

Q: Can it be used on several glands?

A: Yes, several areas or glands. I wouldn't use more than nine stars at once, though.

Q: How often can a diabetic use it for the pancreas?

A: Again, don't overuse it. In the case of diabetes, I think three times a week would be good.

Q: For dizziness, where would you put the star?

A: I'd put it directly below the right ear, right at the jaw or mandibles. I'd also put one across each eyebrow so that you catch the sinus and in the inner ear to take care of *labyrinthitis,* which is inflammation of the inner ear. You'd be surprised at how that just sears through, in a good way.

Q: Does the treatment work for alcoholics or drug addicts?

A: Yes, it's very effective for dependencies of any kind. I'd place the star right in the middle of the eyes because, after all, everything starts in the mind. You might also put one on the pancreatic area if you're an alcoholic, since this addiction is often due to some problem with the pancreas or blood sugar.

Q: Can you put it on someone who won't do it for themselves?

A: While that would be nice, this is one thing that's totally yours. You can ask for this treatment to go out to others, but it won't come.

As an aside, you want to be careful that you don't become too involved in others' lives. Unfortunately, mothers—God love them—can be the worst at this, becoming so obsessed with their children's problems that they no longer have a life of their own. They've been taught that they're supposed to be overprotective, hovering birds of prey, which creates all kinds of problems. They wonder why their children are hypertensive and hyperactive and can't breathe. Did you ever watch somebody who couldn't breathe? She's frantically running all over the place.

Q: Can a healer have someone place his own star in meditation?

A: Yes. If your client tells you where his pain is, you'd tell him to visualize the star on that area. Then you'd put your hands on top of where he placed the star. This would give you a double whammy in that you can add your healing energy to his star.

Q: So then we really can use the Star Treatment to heal others?

A: No! You have to use it on yourself and they have to use it on themselves. You can give them the knowledge of the star, but they have to use it—you can't use it on them. The tools I've given you, such as the mirrors of meditation, can be given to anybody. Of course you can't necessarily put mirrors around people and be as effective as if they were doing it themselves. It's much like a vaccination: if two people get sick but only one gets vaccinated, it won't help the person who didn't take it, nor can the vaccinated individual give that treatment to the other person. The Star Treatment is one of the things that's selfishly yours and yours alone—no one can do it for you.

Q: Can we just think of the star if we can't visualize it?

A: Yes, it's the same thing. If you think of the star, and you know what a star looks like, you're already there.

You don't have to have it appear right there in your head, since you know what a star looks like. People have the wrong perception that everybody's supposed to see it in 3-D, glowing color.

Q: What if the mind drifts and you can't concentrate?

A: Keep practicing the technique. If you didn't get your star, keep trying for it—it can simply take time to come to you on occasion.

Q: What about mental or emotional healing?

A: Placing a star right in the center of your forehead will really make your mind calm and peaceful.

Let me show you how marvelously this works by giving you what I call "the Spiritual Laser Star Meditation":

I want you to put your hands upward on your thighs and take a deep breath. Put a golden light around you by visualizing yourself being surrounded by a golden glow of light. If you feel hurt or tired or beaten up by the world, put a silver net or the white light of the Holy Spirit around you and take a deep breath. Feel God's presence around you, know that the true Christ is with you, and feel that Mother God is with you.

Close your eyes . . . in the front of the top part of your eyes, looking up at your forehead, begin to see a velvet black sky, which is dark and seems endless. All of a sudden—moving from left to right until it gets to the middle of your vision, where the apex of your forehead resides, right between your eyebrows—you can see this star. It is very tiny at first, but with a slight squint, you can see that it's silver blue in color.

In a flash, this star becomes bigger, twirling through space until it beams right down on your forehead. It is so bright that you have to keep your physical eyes closed, but it will not hurt them. Eventually your soul eyes get used to it, but it is so brilliant that it almost looks like a spotlight shining on your forehead, and you can practically see the fragments of dust in the air—this is how radiant it is. The longer you look at it, the easier it becomes for you to see it.

You marvel that it becomes glittery, silver, crystal-like, until it is almost opaque in its reflected beauty. As you look, you are beginning to feel it pulsate in the middle of your forehead; it is not an unpleasant feeling, but a slight throbbing and pulsating motion to relax your mind. Let its beams go down through your body, even though you are not addressing those parts of yourself now. You are addressing the mind; you are addressing the crown chakra, the pineal and pituitary glands. It is riveting into them all.

Feel the quiet peace. As this star is penetrating your mind with the blessedness of grace, goodness, and positive energy, feel yourself become renewed, almost as if you're shedding some old skin—the old fears, the old frights. All the things that you thought were important begin to fall away . . . all the old paranoias, the indecisions. It seems as if with each thing you shed, whether it is a phobia or a problem— the star pulsates more strongly, so in its strength it washes the negative away. The star is getting rid of everything negative in your mind and the darkness from the world outside. Yet you are always keeping your own identity, your own self, and you are always keeping control.

Feel yourself letting go with a great breath. At this moment, ask for the most pivotal thing that is important to you, which is going to give you energy, motivation, or health—anything that has to do with the physical body, the mental body, and the soul.

With the quiet peace around you, begin to bring yourself up to full consciousness, feeling absolutely marvelous, better than you have ever felt before. On the count of three, bring yourself all the way up: one, two, three.

The star is such a powerful archetypical symbol, and it has been throughout all time. When you use this meditation, you can heat up, but you will not be harmed; neither will the brightness of the star or the tingling and pulsation that you feel hurt you.

Q: Isn't there a healing technique called "the Lab," where we call on Master Healers and others on the Other Side?

A: Yes, and it's a very effective healing technique that requires two steps.

First, you must eject all negativity: all of the ideas that you're getting older, that age means anything, that you're getting menopausal (whether you're female or male), or that doctors say this is the time of life when "these things" should happen . . . it all has to be driven out of you through positive programming and cell memory. In other words, you first do your cell-memory programming in the morning, using God's help.

Next, go to the Lab at night. The Lab is a technique in which you actually see yourself wheeled into a laboratory: There is a huge, fantastic, stained-glass window above you that's much like a wheel, with panes of purple, green, and gold. You lie on a type of a gurney very quietly and let all of these beautiful purple, green, and gold lights resonate to different parts of your chakras (the openings of the body that correspond to your different glands). While lying there, ask the Master Teachers and doctors from the Other Side to come and administer to you to facilitate a healing.

Say, "As I lie here, I request to have all of the Master Teachers, healers, technicians, and doctors come work on me." You'll be quite amazed when you do this, even if you can't visualize it in the beginning. You'll immediately start to feel that there's a certain heat or warmth that begins to emanate out of one or more parts of your body.

A woman recently told Sylvia that when she did the Lab technique, she felt extra warmth in her bladder and thought, *That's amazing.* The next day, however, she came down with a urinary infection. She couldn't get an appointment with her doctor right away, so she went to bed that night and mentally sent more heat to the affected area. By the time she was able to go see her doctor three days later, her bladder was cured.

The Other Side's guides, healers, and Master Teachers were alerting her that there was a problem before her consciousness even knew it. They were working on her before the onset of something serious—so all she got was the minor irritation, and then it was healed.

So if you feel a certain area becoming very warm when you go to the Lab, don't be concerned about it. If it's your chest, don't say, "Oh my God, I'm having a heart attack!" Certainly you must always go to the doctor and have anything unusual checked, but you might find that the Other Side is healing you before you even know that something is wrong. Sometimes they're much more aware of your body than you are, which is nice to know—that's preventive and an insurance policy.

Q: Could you give us a prayer utilizing all these tools?

A: What we've found on my side is that people don't want to spend two to five minutes to upgrade their health, spirituality, and happiness. They think that's too much . . . yet they'll spend hours on their hair, picking their clothes out, or sitting in front of a screen watching something that's of no purpose or importance in their life. To spare a few minutes each day or even a couple of times a week is too much for protection, meditation, visualization, and health employing cell memory and the mind.

For those of you who *do* want to take a few minutes to help yourself, put the white light of the Holy Spirit around you when you get up in the morning and ask that any negativity that comes to you be absorbed into the light so that it doesn't affect you. If you can't visualize iridescent white light surrounding you, then just ask for it to come. The more active your mental process or your verbalization is, the more it becomes a reality. Get a picture of yourself and draw a rainbow or bubble of light around it for something tangible to look at in the morning. (I always like to give the example of Glinda the Good Witch in *The Wizard of Oz* arriving in her bubble of light as a good visual.)

Next, state: "Anything that I've carried over that's negative to my cell memory, I want to be absolved, dissipated, released, and absorbed by the white light. Any wonderful, energetic, full-of-youth, healthy, vital cell memory that I can bring up from any age and any time, I do so now!" It's very good if you can pick a specific time in your life to focus on, but if you can't, then leave it up to the archangels and your angels to choose it for you. You'll be surprised at how an age will suddenly spring to mind.

This happened to a woman Sylvia was working with: she got the age of 17 as her optimal "time," and from that point on, she began using that cell memory of 17. Her leg was once frozen at the knee, but now she has perfect movement because she demanded that the central location of the mind—the limbic brain—activate. (The primitive, limbic brain is always a good place to start with cell memory.)

Once you've established your optimal time of health, energy, and vitality, address the mind and say, "I demand that the cell memory come up from the age of 17 [or whatever it may be] and that my deductive and inductive reasoning become even better with each moment, each day, and each year."

When you begin to bring this cell memory up, you'll realize that when you were 17, you didn't have the arthritic pains or whatever problem you're dealing with now. The mind will go in accordance with that, and it will believe you. So what's even more important than nutrition, exercise, and all the lotions that you put on your face or your body is what you tell your mind. Your mind is the creative force that God has given to you down here, and your body will always follow its lead.

Also, be cognizant of what people call "age spots" as you get older. We are convinced that none of this is due to aging as much as it has to do with cell memory. So if you see a new spot on your face developing, it might be wise to tell yourself, "Whatever I'm doing or have done that has created this, or whatever bad situation might have happened at this age and time in a prior existence, I release it!" If your mind doesn't resonate to it, your body will.

And when it comes to the loss of memory as you age, it doesn't have to be this way! The more you train your mind, the more it stays strong, since it's a muscle that can be exercised. Once you discipline your mind and focus it on your truth—not my truth, but *your* truth—then the spirit gets well, the soul gets well, the mind gets well, and everything begins to shine to the point that you have fewer problems.

☙ ☙ ☙ ☙ ☙ ☙

Afterword

As you can see, optimal wellness is available for anyone who wishes it. Whether you're trying to cure yourself of a physical illness or disease, or you're just attempting to be a better person and live a better life, it's the effort that you put into healing yourself that will ultimately determine whether that healing is going to take place.

I must reiterate here that some entities choose to be sick in this life for their own learning process; in other words, it's in their chart. If you're one of those who has chosen to write illness of some sort in your chart, that doesn't mean you'll be unable to alleviate it or lessen its impact on your life. It's certainly worth trying the tools for healing that my spirit guides and I have given you in this book, for you might be pleasantly surprised by what they can do for you. And for those of you who are impacted by another person's affliction, there's nothing to prevent you from trying these methods out on them—they certainly won't make the situation worse.

Healing can sometimes be a long and slow process, so don't get discouraged and start to slack off. You'll notice improvement if you keep at it, and you may even be completely healed. Even when it comes to those of you who have a terminal illness of some sort, the extension of your life is entirely in your hands. If doctors have said that you're going to die, activate your will and use the methods in these pages to obtain that healing you so desire, *and as long as your will to live remains intact, you will not die.*

Francine and Raheim have given us all some good insights into areas of healing that have been heretofore unexplored by conventional medicine; unconventional or not, if they work, who cares? You should always look into all methods of healing, especially if you've been given a death sentence; after all, it can't make things worse than they already are. Take supplements, go on a special diet if you have to, research holistic publications, explore new methods of treatment that may not be available in your country . . . do anything and everything you need to do to stay alive and keep that will to live intact.

I was reading the other day about a new noninvasive treatment for certain types of cancer that they're doing in Ireland. It entails using a light-attracting substance that's injected into the cancerous area, and then lasers are used from outside the body to kill off cancer cells, which seem to have more of an affinity for this substance than healthy cells do. The substance draws the laser beam into the cancer cells and kills them, with little effect upon healthy tissue. I don't have the full story on this, but there are many such new and experimental treatments being tried for various diseases throughout the world that I certainly would explore if I had such a health issue.

New treatments and inhibitors are being started every day on illness and disease. While not all of them are successful, some are —so find any and every option you may have. I certainly believe in the techniques detailed in the preceding pages (otherwise I never would have given them out), but you must understand that any healing method is only as good as the person doing it. If you don't give full effort to it and believe in it with all your heart and soul, the method may not be as effective as it would be for someone who faithfully, and with will and passion, uses it to achieve wellness. You have the power of God within you to heal yourself from any illness or disease . . . you just have to activate it!

Finally, I'd like to mention the Other Side's Hall of Healing, which can be accessed through meditation for advanced curative effects. (Please see my book *Temples on the Other Side* for further explanation on this hall and a meditation to help you reach it.) For example, when you visit this magnificent building, Mother God will give you a powerful phrase that simply means "Evil be gone!" but consists of words not known to us on Earth. Francine has tried to research the origins of these words and found that they're so ancient she can't even find how far back they go. But if you go to the temple regularly and have the statue of the Mother God bless you and utilize those words, you'll find that your life is more protected from evil of any kind, for nothing is more powerful as a protective tool.

Keeping yourself in good health and in a positive frame of mind is key to living a happier life, but you'll find that such an attitude allows you to do more for others, too. I know that it can be hard to find the time, energy, and will to make yourself a better person; but when you get down on yourself, remember that both Father and Mother God are there for you in a constantly loving and protective embrace . . . this life is only a temporary state of existence, and all things shall pass.

God love you. I do.
Sylvia

❧ ❧ ❧   ❧ ❧ ❧

About the Author

Sylvia Browne is the #1 *New York Times* best-selling author and world-famous psychic medium who appears regularly on *The Montel Williams Show* and *Larry King Live,* as well as making countless other media and public appearances. With her down-to-earth personality and great sense of humor, Sylvia thrills audiences on her lecture tours and still has time to write numerous immensely popular books. She has a master's degree in English literature and plans to write as long as she can hold a pen.

Sylvia is the president of the Sylvia Browne Corporation; and is the founder of her church, the Society of Novus Spiritus, located in Campbell, California. Please contact her at: **www.sylvia.org**, or call **(408) 379-7070** for further information about her work. Sylvia is also featured on an additional Website: **www.SpiritNow.com**.

❧ ❧ ❧   ❧ ❧ ❧

Hay House Titles of Related Interest

YOU CAN HEAL YOUR LIFE, the movie,
starring Louise L. Hay & Friends
(available as a 1-DVD program and an expanded 2-DVD set)
Watch the trailer at: **www.LouiseHayMovie.com**

THE SHIFT, the movie,
starring Dr. Wayne W. Dyer
(available as a 1-DVD program and an expanded 2-DVD set)
Watch the trailer at: **www.DyerMovie.com**

❀ ❀ ❀

**THE ART OF EXTREME SELF-CARE: Transform Your Life
One Month at a Time,** by Cheryl Richardson

**THE ASTONISHING POWER OF EMOTIONS:
Let Your Feelings Be Your Guide,** by Esther and Jerry Hicks
(The Teachings of Abraham®)

**THE BODY KNOWS . . . HOW TO STAY YOUNG: Healthy-Aging
Secrets from a Medical Intuitive,** by Caroline Sutherland

**THE INTUITIVE ADVISOR: A Psychic Doctor Teaches You
How to Solve Your Most Pressing Health Problems,**
by Mona Lisa Schulz, M.D., Ph.D.

**IT'S THE THOUGHT THAT COUNTS: Why Mind Over Matter
Really Works,** by David R. Hamilton, Ph.D.

**MIND PROGRAMMING: From Persuasion and Brainwashing to
Self-Help and Practical Metaphysics** (book-with-CD),
by Eldon Taylor

REPETITION: Past Lives, Life, and Rebirth,
by Doris Eliana Cohen, Ph.D.

**RETURN TO THE SACRED: Ancient Pathways to Spiritual
Awakening,** by Jonathan H. Ellerby, Ph.D.

YOU CAN HEAL YOUR LIFE, by Louise L. Hay

❀ ❀ ❀

All of the above are available at your local bookstore,
or may be ordered by contacting Hay House (see next page).

❀ ❀ ❀

We hope you enjoyed this Hay Housebook.
If you'd like to receive our online catalog featuring additional
information on Hay House books and products, or if you'd like to
find out more about the Hay Foundation, please contact:

Hay House, Inc.
P.O. Box 5100
Carlsbad, CA 92018-5100

(760) 431-7695 or **(800) 654-5126**
(760) 431-6948 (fax) or **(800) 650-5115 (fax)**
www.hayhouse.com® • **www.hayfoundation.org**

☙ ☙ ☙

Published and distributed in Australia by:
Hay House Australia Pty. Ltd., 18/36 Ralph St., Alexandria NSW 2015
Phone: 612-9669-4299 • *Fax:* 612-9669-4144 • www.hayhouse.com.au

Published and distributed in the United Kingdom by:
Hay House UK, Ltd., 292B Kensal Rd., London W10 5BE
Phone: 44-20-8962-1230 • *Fax:* 44-20-8962-1239 • www.hayhouse.co.uk

Published and distributed in the Republic of South Africa by:
Hay House SA (Pty), Ltd., P.O. Box 990, Witkoppen 2068
Phone/Fax: 27-11-467-8904 • info@hayhouse.co.za
www.hayhouse.co.za

Published in India by: Hay House Publishers India, Muskaan Complex,
Plot No. 3, B-2, Vasant Kunj, New Delhi 110 070
Phone: 91-11-4176-1620 • *Fax:* 91-11-4176-1630 • www.hayhouse.co.in

Distributed in Canada by: Raincoast, 9050 Shaughnessy St., Vancouver,
B.C. V6P 6E5 • *Phone:* (604) 323-7100 • *Fax:* (604) 323-2600
www.raincoast.com

☙ ☙ ☙

Take Your Soul on a Vacation

Visit **www.HealYourLife.com**® to regroup, recharge, and reconnect
with your own magnificence. Featuring blogs, mind-body-spirit news,
and life-changing wisdom from Louise Hay and friends.

Visit **www.HealYourLife.com** today!